DR. RUTH'S GUIDE TO SAFER SEX

takes the fear out of being close – for everybody!

- Practical advice about prevention and pleasure for straight, gay and lesbian people
- The pleasure of giving pleasure – and how to make it work for safer sex
- Creative masturbation – and how it not only affords protection but makes intimate times even more fun
- Changing a man's mind about condoms, from avoidance to eagerness
- How to make sex a more caring, joy-filled activity for both men and women, even in the years of AIDS – until a cure is found.

DR RUTH WESTHEIMER, psychosexual therapist, pioneered the field of media psychology in America with her radio show, *Sexually Speaking*, in 1980. Today, her television shows – 'The Dr. Ruth Show', 'What's Up, Dr. Ruth?', 'You're on the Air with Dr. Ruth', and her new programme, 'Never Too Late' on Nostalgia Television – have won a wide audience and prestigious awards. She conducts her own private practice, serves on the faculties of New York University and is a fellow of the New York Academy of Medicine, and lectures and holds seminars across the United States. She reaches a worldwide readership with her advice column, 'Ask Dr. Ruth', syndicated by King Features. She is the author of seven books including *Dr. Ruth's Guide to Good Sex*, *First Love*, *Dr. Ruth's Guide for Married Lovers*, her autobiography *All in a Lifetime*, and, now, DR RUTH'S GUIDE TO SAFER SEX.

DR. RUTH'S GUIDE TO SAFER SEX

DR. RUTH WESTHEIMER

B🌱XTREE

I dedicate this book to all the researchers and contributors who are involved in finding a way for safer sex in these troubled times.

This edition published by arrangement with Warner Books, Inc., New York

First published in the UK 1992 by BOXTREE LIMITED, Broadwall House, 21 Broadwall, London SE1 9PL

10 9 8 7 6 5 4 3 2 1

Copyright © 1992 Dr. Ruth Westheimer

All rights reserved. Except for use in a review, no part of this book may be reproduced, stored in a retrieval system or transmitted in any form or by any means, electronic, mechanical, photocopying, recording or otherwise, without prior permission of Boxtree Ltd.

Front cover photograph by Erik Heinila

Typeset by D P Photosetting
Printed and bound in Great Britain by
Cox & Wyman Ltd, Reading, Berkshire

ISBN 1-85283-430-7

A CIP catalogue entry for this book is available from the British Library

Foremost in my mind when it is time to thank my family and many friends for their loyal support in all my endeavours, is my special friend and writer Ben Yagoda. He, in turn, thanks his wife Gigi Simeone, his two daughters, Elizabeth and Maria, his mother, Harriet Yagoda, and the AIDS Library of Philadelphia for valuable research and assistance.

So that I don't have to add another chapter, I will express my heartfelt gratitude to some who have had a particularly important role in my work: Maria Cuadrado, Helen Singer Kaplan, M.D., Ph.D., Rabbi Leonard Kravitz, Rabbi Robert Lehman, Pierre Lehu, Professor Louis Lieberman, John Lollos, and John Silberman.

Also, Susan Suffes, a superbly helpful, encouraging, and skillful editor, and Larry Kirshbaum and William Sarnoff at Warner Books.

CONTENTS

Daughters of Jerusalem,
I charge you:
don't stir up,
don't rouse love
until it be ready!

– Song of Songs,
Chapter 8, Verse 4

INTRODUCTION

About ten years ago, I was working on my first book, *Dr. Ruth's Guide to Good Sex*. I thought I should include a section on sexually transmitted disease, so I did an interview with my friend Dr. Jack Forest, a noted urologist. At the end of the interview, he mentioned that there were a number of new diseases in evidence.

'Among them is Kaposi's sarcoma,' he said. 'For years it was known as an endemic disease in Africa, almost entirely limited to women. They would get big purple malignant spots on the legs and lower torso. A minority of cases were fatal when it was involved in the bloodstream and the liver. But few people died from it. In the last few years, however, we have come across Kaposi's sarcoma in almost epidemic proportions and almost entirely limited to gay men, and it is related statistically to the number of partners they have and the amount of anal intercourse.

1

'All we know at this time,' he concluded, 'is that it is epidemic, limited to gay men, and related to the frequency of anal sex with different partners.'

Even though some people advised me not to include the quote in the book – it was too remote from most readers' lives, they said – I left it in. I thought the information was important.

Little did I know how important it was. As the book was going to press, it was recognised in the medical community that the Kaposi's sarcoma Dr. Forest was speaking of was just a symptom of a far more serious disease. This was called acquired immune deficiency syndrome – AIDS. At first it was concentrated in the gay community and among intravenous drug users, but as the decade progressed, it was seen in non-I.V.-using heterosexuals as well. To date, more than 200,000 people in the United States alone have been diagnosed as having AIDS. It is caused by a virus called HIV that is transmitted through the exchange of blood and semen and possibly some other bodily fluids and has proved to be extremely resistant to any vaccine. As far as doctors know, AIDS is always fatal.

I can't pinpoint the exact date when I first became aware of how serious the problem was. I do know when the horror really hit home. It was when three friends of mine became victims of AIDS. The first was a superb mental-health worker. Very shortly after he was diagnosed as having the disease, he died, leaving both his patients and his friends, all of whom had come to depend on him, feeling terribly alone.

The second case showed me how emotionally complicated AIDS can be. Two friends of mine were gay lovers, both professors, who had been together for fifteen years. I'll call them Frank and Edward. Frank went to Paris on a teaching assignment. While he was there, he had an affair and was infected with HIV. Then, before he knew about it, he infected Edward. When Frank became sick, Edward took care of him with incredible tenderness and care. Eventually, of course, they both died.

Even I, who have always been kidded about my relentlessly upbeat outlook, am depressed by this horrible disease. Lately I've caught myself looking at the obituary page of *The New York Times*, scanning the ages of the people who've died. When they're young, I look at the second paragraphs, where the cause of death is given. Far, far too often, it is AIDS.

I am fortunate enough to have been married to the same (need I say wonderful?) man for over thirty years, so I don't worry about contracting AIDS myself. But what about my single friends? I know the anxiety they feel – they're aware that, as far as AIDS go, whenever they go to bed with someone, they're going to bed with everybody that person has ever gone to bed with. They feel that if the possibility of sex arises they have to pull out a clipboard and pencil and do an in-depth interview, which is not exactly the most romantic thing in the world. I've spent my whole career talking about the pleasures of sex. Now, whenever I see the *word* sex, my immediate thought is, *For people with no steady partner, this is a difficult time*.

But doom and gloom won't help defeat the AIDS epidemic. (That's true for everybody, not just upbeat folks like me.) So let me, as I always like to do, look on the bright side. It took a long time, but the American public – prodded by such factors as the death of Rock Hudson in 1986, the release of former Surgeon General Everett Koop's report on AIDS in 1987, and basketball hero Magic Johnson's announcement in 1991 that he had been infected with HIV even though he's heterosexual – has finally begun to comprehend the enormity of the problem, and the fact that everyone is affected, not just gay men and drug users.

Another positive development is the fact that, using a variety of strategies and techniques, it has been shown to be possible for individuals to substantially reduce their risk of getting AIDS. This is called 'safer sex', and that is what this book is all about. Gay men were the first to be hit by AIDS, and they were the first to embrace safer sex. As a result, AIDS rates in the gay community have gone steadily down over the past few years.

Gays and others have shown that safer sex doesn't have to be dull sex. In the pages that follow, along with nuts-and-bolts information about risks and ways to avoid them, you'll find advice on how to make an omelette out of broken eggs. In other words, how to take the rules of safer sex and use them to concoct a more exciting, more creative, sexier life than you had before.

I've found in my sex-therapy practice and my talks with people from all walks of life, all around the country, that the threat of AIDS, and the resultant emphasis on safer sex, has had at least one definite positive effect: because the *least* safe sex is vaginal or anal intercourse, many lovers have been encouraged to get to know each other and each other's bodies, to discover sensuous spots that might otherwise not be found, to spend more *time* with each other. They've had to use their imagination and their creativity. Before, maybe there was too much of a concentration on one specific act. And believe me, there's a lot more to sex than intercourse.

But before I get too carried away, let me close this introduction on a cautionary note. Safer sex is just that – safer, not safe. Even before I became aware of the magnitude of the AIDS threat, I used the term 'safer sex' to refer to contraception. I knew that no method was 100 percent effective: the rhythm method was fraught with peril; IUDs, the diaphragm, and the pill all had their failure rates; condoms could break, slip off, or be used improperly.

So it is with sexually transmitted diseases (of which AIDS is, of course, only one). The only truly safe forms of sex are abstinence and mutual monogamy with an uninfected partner. Everything else carries with it some degree of risk. It has been disheartening, moreover, to see some backsliding to unsafe practices in the gay community, to see that even after Magic Johnson's announcement, there is still an appalling rate of ignorance about AIDS in this country and, among many people, a frightful willingness to engage in extremely risky behaviour.

I know very well that doctors are working frantically on developing an AIDS vaccine. Until they are successful, we all have a moral obligation to be as careful as we possibly can be.

And that's what safer sex is all about.

CHAPTER I

The Problem: HIV and AIDS

If a screenwriter had proposed the idea in 1980, it would have been rejected out of hand. Think of it: a mysterious, fatal disease is spread from Africa to the United States. The main means of transmission, it develops, is sexual intimacy. At first it affects only homosexuals, but then it appears in the heterosexual community as well. The man who was once considered the handsomest movie star in the country dies of it; the most popular basketball player announces he is infected. Scientists feverishly work at a cure, but to no avail. Within a decade, there are over 200,000 cases in the U.S. – more than 100,000 of them fatal – and some 1.5 million worldwide.

As the decade progressed, the disease became no less improbable or deadly, but a good deal less mysterious. Scientists called it acquired immune deficiency syndrome, or AIDS, because it destroyed the body's natural system of immunity to disease. People don't die of AIDS itself. Rather, once it has set in, they become extremely susceptible to other diseases, and usually die within a few years, most commonly of a form of pneumonia referred to as PCP or a rare kind of cancer, Kaposi's sarcoma, that produces purplish lesions on the skin. (PCP is now preventable, an example of the advances made in the fight against AIDS.)

In 1984, researchers in the United States and France simultaneously identified the virus that causes AIDS. This virus, now referred to as HIV (for human immune deficiency virus), invades white blood cells (known as T-4 cells) that play an essential role in the immune system. HIV is what is known as a retrovirus, meaning that it reproduces only in living cells. One of the things that makes it so difficult to fight is that each time the host cell divides, copies of the virus are produced, each containing the genetic code of HIV. When HIV reproduces, it destroys the infected T-4 cell. AIDS develops when there are so few T-4 cells left that infection cannot be fought off.

The Centers for Disease Control recently estimated that one million people in the United States are infected with HIV, with 40,000 new infections a year. Throughout the world, there are 9 to 11 million cases, according to the World Health Organization. WHO predicts that by the year 2000, that figure will be 40 million.

What makes these figures especially frightening is that many people have HIV but are not aware of it. Before the onset of AIDS, people with HIV may show no symptoms at all, or only relatively minor, non-life-threatening ones like fevers, chronic fatigue, or diarrhoea. One recent study found that the average length of time between HIV infection and the development of AIDS is eight to eleven years. It may be possible, in fact, to get HIV and *never* get AIDS; scientists still aren't sure.

But they *are* sure that anyone with HIV is capable of passing the virus on to others, through sexual contact or by sharing needles. This fact alone to some extent justifies some of the hysteria that AIDS has spawned. Only a terribly irresponsible person would knowingly expose a sex partner to the risk of HIV. But what if someone has the virus without knowing it? He or she could be a nice person, pay all their bills on time, always say please and thank you – could be, in fact, a universally loved celebrity like Magic Johnson – and still be the carrier of a deadly disease. If that person is your sex partner, you are at risk.

OTHER STDS

All of the sound and fury about HIV and AIDS has tended to obscure the fact that a whole depressing lineup of other sexually transmitted diseases (STDs) is still out there. Thanks in part to the spread of the good news about abstinence and safer sex, STDs have recently shown a decline: there were 14.5 percent fewer syphilis cases in America in 1991 than in 1990, and 10 percent fewer gonorrhea cases. Even so, STDs strike an estimated 12 million Americans every year, including 3 million teenagers. While AIDS is the big gun for obvious reasons – it cannot be cured and it is fatal – it behoves everyone to be informed about the other STDs. Here's a lineup:

Syphilis. Caused by a bacterium that invades the mucous membranes of the mouth, rectum, and vagina, syphilis first shows up – within six weeks of infection – in the form of genital lesions called chancres. These are followed within a few months by such symptoms as fevers, aches, rashes, hair loss, mouth sores, and, eventually, if the disease is left untreated, by serious damage to the heart, brain, eyes, and other organs. Syphilis can be passed by a pregnant woman to her unborn baby.

Fortunately, syphilis can be treated with

antibiotics. *Unfortunately*, despite the decline in 1991, syphilis has been on the upswing in America, with reported cases doubling in the years since 1984, to an annual incidence of well over 100,000 cases. Alarmingly, the rate among black males is fifty-four times higher than it is among whites.

Gonorrhea. Gonorrhea is caused by a bacterium so infectious that it can be passed on by simple genital contact, even when there's no penetration. It results in genital itching or burning or unusual discharges, usually within two to ten days of infection. If untreated by antibiotics, it can cause pelvic inflammatory disease (PID) in women, which can lead to infertility or ectopic pregnancy.

In the United States the number of gonorrhea cases declined steadily throughout the 1980s, but there are still more than one million reported cases a year.

Chlamydia. The most common sexually transmitted disease, with an estimated 4 million cases annually in America, chlamydia is a bacterial infection whose symptoms include painful urination and, in women, vaginal discharge and general pain in the lower abdomen. Like gonorrhea, it can lead to PID.

What makes chlamydia particularly tricky is that a quarter of the infected men and half of

the infected women never experience any
symptoms. So some doctors recommend that
anyone with more than one sex partner –
especially women who plan to have children –
be tested once a year.

Genital herpes. In the days before AIDS,
herpes got a lot of publicity. The publicity went
away, but the problem is still there.

More than 30 million Americans have the
disease, a figure that is growing at a rate of
500,000 a year. A virus rather than a bacterium,
herpes is transmitted during intercourse or oral
sex. Within ten days of infection, lesions,
similar to cold sores, appear in the genital
areas. They heal within a few weeks, but the
relief is deceptive. Like HIV, herpes cannot be
cured, and the lesions can reappear without
warning at any moment. Anyone with an active
lesion can pass the disease on to a sex partner.

Hepatitis B. The hepatitis B virus attacks the
liver. Although some people recover naturally
and develop an immunity to further infection
(while still being able to pass the infection on to
sex partners), others can develop liver cancer or
cirrhosis. An estimated 300,000 cases are
contracted every year in the United States,
leading to 5,000 deaths.

The virus is present in the saliva, as well as in
blood, semen, and vaginal secretions, so it can

theoretically be spread by deep, or French, kissing.

There is no cure for hepatitis B, and indeed in some samples, as many as 60 percent of the gay men sampled have been found to test positive. There is, however, a safe and effective vaccine, which the government recommends for all sexually active gay men and all heterosexuals with more than one partner. Gays have by and large heeded the advice, while less than one percent of the heterosexuals at risk have received the vaccine.

Genital warts. These hard, fleshy bumps are caused by a virus that infects an estimated one million Americans a year. The warts themselves can be medically removed, but it's possible that even after removal the condition can lead to cancers of the penis, vulva, and cervix.

Everything I say about safer sex in the course of this book applies to the sexually transmitted diseases described above; as with HIV, the main preventive weapons are, first, abstinence from intercourse, oral-genital and oral-anal contact, and, second, the use of condoms. However, there are some preventive measures for the other STDs that don't really apply to HIV.

1. Contraceptive foams, creams and jellies can help to kill STD bacteria and viruses.
2. Washing the genitals before intercourse

can help remove bacteria.

3. Urinating before and after intercourse can help keep the bacteria out of the urethra.

4. Unlike the HIV virus, many of the STDs have visible signs. If you see a chancre, a wart, a herpes blister, or any discharge in or around the genitals of any potential partner, do not have sex with that person. If you have had sex with the person before, make an appointment with your doctor for an STD examination.

THE FACTS ABOUT HIV AND AIDS

The terrible nature of AIDS makes it critically important that people know the facts – and the fictions – about how HIV is transmitted. Let's start with the fictions. HIV is not spread by casual contact, by which I mean hugging, touching, and even closer contact. Several studies have been done of families in which one member has HIV or AIDS; no one in them was found ever to have been infected by HIV, even though they have shared beds, dishes, clothing, toilets, food, toothbrushes, toys, and baby bottles. (However, sharing items such as toothbrushes and razor blades, on which some blood may be present, is not a very good idea.)

But if this kind of thing concerns you, you

may be relieved to know that, outside the body, HIV is a fairly fragile virus. It can be killed by soap and water, household bleach, hydrogen peroxide, alcohol, Lysol, or swimming-pool chlorine.

Some bodily fluids, such as saliva, tears, perspiration, and urine, could carry small amounts of the virus, but there has never been a documented case where the disease was passed by means of these substances. You can't get it by being sneezed on. This brings up a question I'm almost always asked when I talk about AIDS: What about French kissing? To repeat, HIV has been shown to be present in saliva, but at very low levels, and there has never been an incident of HIV's being passed by French, German, English, or any other kind of kissing. (However, as noted earlier, there is a slight chance of transmitting the hepatitis B virus through kissing.) Should you engage in deep kissing with someone who is HIV positive or whose HIV status you don't know? I'm afraid that the answer, as is too often the case when dealing with AIDS, has to be a vague one: You must use your own judgment.

Finally, AIDS cannot be transmitted by mosquitoes or any other kind of insect. In tests carried out in a Florida town, where mosquitoes had been blamed for a high incidence of AIDS, no one under the age of ten was found to be infected. Mosquitoes do not practise age discrimination. Moreover, it turned out that the vast majority of the people who were infected had a history of high-risk behaviour – they were homosexuals or intravenous drug users, or had sex partners who were.

TRANSMISSION

How *can* HIV be passed from one person to another? The answer is relatively simple. It is spread through the passing of bodily fluids – blood, semen, and possibly secretions of the cervix and vagina – containing the HIV virus from an infected to an uninfected person. (It may also be passed from a mother to a child during pregnancy or birth.) These fluids may be exchanged in a limited number of ways: by anal or genital sexual intercourse or oral sex; by receiving contaminated blood; or by using a contaminated hypodermic needle.

This is a book about safer sex, so the second and third ways are beyond its scope. Before moving on, though, let me say a word about them. Since 1985, the supply of blood used for transfusion in the U.S. has been screened for contamination, as it is in many other countries, so it poses only infinitesimal hazards. If you received blood between 1978 and 1985, you may wish to be tested for HIV. I will discuss the issue in the next chapter. (There is not now and there never has been any danger in *giving* blood.) If you are an intravenous drug user, never, *never*, share needles.

How are these fluids exchanged during sex? Again, in a limited number of ways. HIV can enter the body if contaminated blood or semen comes in contact with open sores or wounds in the mouth, vagina, or rectum, or also through the mucous membranes that line the vagina, rectum, urethra, and possibly the mouth. Some experts consider anal sex to be riskier than genital sex because of the greater possibility that blood or open wounds will be present in the anus or rectum.

The vulnerability of the urethra is significant, incidentally, because it explains something that often puzzles people: how men can become infected in the process of anal or genital intercourse. Contaminated blood or vaginal or cervical secretions can enter their bloodstreams through the opening of the penis.

THE RISKS

Just as a single act of intercourse between a man and woman does not necessarily mean that the woman will become pregnant, a single act of sex with an infected person does not necessarily mean that you will become infected yourself. In San Francisco, where the disease has reached epidemic proportions, a random sample of gay men in 1987 found that fully 29 percent of those who reported having more than fifty partners during the previous two years nevertheless tested negative for HIV. (The number would have been much higher, to be sure, if the message of safer sex hadn't been widely spread in San Francisco.) Still, one sexual episode is sufficient to spread the virus, and those who have unprotected sex, especially with partners who they know to have practised high-risk behaviours (anal sex, IV-drug use, sex with many partners) are practising a late-twentieth-century form of Russian roulette.

Since the majority of people in this world are heterosexual, the question of the risk of HIV transmission through straight sex is naturally a pressing one. Unfortunately, the answer – or answers – are not particularly straightforward. To start, the disease definitely can be spread through heterosexual intercourse. In the U.S., about 12,000 AIDS cases have been transmitted this way, which works out to approximately 6 percent of the total. Transmission of HIV has been reported after only one sexual contact with an infected partner. On the other hand, some people have remained uninfected after hundreds of contacts.

There are several explanations for the

disparity. It is possible that some strains of HIV are more transmissible than others, that infectiousness varies over the course of the HIV infection, and that some people are more susceptible than others. In addition, there appears to be a correlation between suscept-ibility to HIV and the presence of other sexually transmitted diseases, such as syphilis, genital herpes, gonorrhea, and chlamydia, in part because the open oral and general sores that these diseases create are veritable gateways for HIV. Finally, people who smoke crack have been shown to be extremely susceptible. Not only does the practice cause drying and chapping around the mouth, making it easier for the virus to enter the body during oral sex, but crack users are notorious for exchanging sexual favours for the drug. Each sexual encounter increases the risk of becoming infected.

Both women and men can get the disease from heterosexual intercourse, although women appear to be at significantly greater risk. One recent study found that 20 percent of the women who were long-term sex partners of infected men were themselves infected, as opposed to only 1.4 percent (one of seventy-two) of the men who were long-term partners of infected women.

OTHER KINDS OF SEX

What I've said so far applies to sexual intercourse. Some other kinds of sexual behaviour have their own risks. In addition to genital or anal intercourse without a condom, oral sex carries with it some degree of risk for both straights and gays – a risk that is substantially increased for the person performing the oral sex if there are cuts or sores or bleeding gums in his or her mouth.

Fellatio – commonly referred to as a blow job – is considered high-risk if the man ejaculates into his partner's mouth; HIV virus present in the semen can be absorbed into the bloodstream through the mucous membranes in the mouth, or through small tears or cuts in the lining of the mouth, stomach, or gastrointestinal tract. (But it probably can't be absorbed through the digestive system – the HIV virus seems to be inactivated by digestive acids and enzymes in the stomach.) But you're not out of the woods even if the penis is withdrawn before ejaculation. It is possible that the pre-ejaculatory fluid ('pre-cum') of an infected person can contain the virus, in which case the person performing the fellatio could become infected. It is less risky if the tip of the penis is not taken into the mouth, and least risky of all if a condom is used. For more about condoms, see Chapter III.

Cunnilingus – or oral sex performed upon a woman – during menstruation is high-risk because of the presence of the virus in menstrual blood. Although it's somewhat less risky when the woman receiving it is not menstruating, vaginal and cervical secretions of an infected person contain some concentration of the virus, so there is still some risk. This is considerably lowered if a barrier, such as a 'dental dam', is used to separate the genitals from the mouth of the partner. I'll discuss dental dams at more length in Chapter III.

Oral-anal contact ('rimming') is dangerous because blood may be present in the anus or rectum. The hepatitis B virus can also be transmitted this way. As with cunnilingus, the risks associated with rimming can be greatly reduced if a dental dam is used.

There is currently some controversy in the gay community about exactly how unsafe unprotected oral sex is. There definitely is some risk. However, only a handful of cases of HIV transmission through oral sex have been documented, leading some to conclude that the risk is extremely low. My opinion? Any risk is too much.

The breast milk of an HIV-positive woman has been shown to contain the virus, so it's possible to become infected by sucking the breasts of an infected, lactating woman.

RECENT DEVELOPMENTS

Since the identification of AIDS in the early 1980s and the widespread dissemination of information about the disease, there's been some good news and some bad news. The good news won't take very long to relate, so I'll start with it. Some people responded admirably to the warnings about the dangers of AIDS, most notably the American gay community. The incredibly creative and resourceful work of such organisations as the Gay Men's Health Crisis in New York, the San Francisco AIDS Foundation, and AIDS Project Los Angeles have provided a model for how to fight an epidemic through education and self-help.

One study showed that high-risk behaviour among gay men in San Francisco had decreased 90 percent between 1978 and 1985 – obviously because many people had taken the message of safer sex to heart. As a result, the rate of new HIV infection among gay men in the city dropped steadily through the decade.

In 1987, it was predicted that there would be 291,000 AIDS cases in this country by the end of 1991. The actual figure turned out to be almost 100,000 less than that, the shortfall certainly having a great deal to do with the adoption of safer sex practices by the gay community. In 1991, the number of diagnosed AIDS cases in the United States actually went *down*, from nearly 39,000 in 1990 to less than 31,000 – the first time that has happened since the disease began to be reported in 1981.

It took a long time, but there were indications that Magic Johnson's announcement in the fall of 1991 brought about some heartening – if not necessarily permanent – changes in attitude and behaviour in the heterosexual community. Suddenly, people realised that there was a difference between AIDS and HIV, and that a straight, non-IV-using, otherwise healthy person could get infected. Even before Johnson's announcement, sex-education programmes in the schools had started to become more extensive and prevalent, and several municipal school systems, including New York, Philadelphia, Portland (Oregon), and San Francisco, have recently announced they would make condoms available to high-school students.

A couple of months after Johnson delivered his bombshell, the Gallup polling organisation asked people how the news about Magic would affect their own behaviour. Here are some of the results.

**WOULD JOHNSON'S
ANNOUNCEMENT MAKE
YOU MORE LIKELY TO:**   **'YES'**

Practise 'safe sex'?   70 percent

Talk with your children about AIDS?	69 percent
Limit the number of sex partners you have?	60 percent
Contribute to an AIDS charity?	59 percent
Have your blood tested to find out if you have the AIDS virus?	41 percent

That's about it for good news. The main bad news, of course, is the continued spread of AIDS and the inability of scientists to come up with a cure. The search for an AIDS vaccine is made immensely more difficult by the fact that HIV has many different shapes and characteristics. Moreover, it mutates rapidly; a vaccine that works against one form of it may not do any good against the others.

AIDS can, to some extent, be controlled. A drug called AZT has been used with some success in people with HIV, stopping the virus from multiplying and delaying the onset of AIDS. Other treatments are being developed, and the hope is that before too long HIV will be a manageable, albeit chronic, illness along the lines of diabetes.

Another line of research is the possibility of developing a 'virucide', a substance that could kill the HIV virus on contact and that a woman could spread in her vagina before having sex.

One problem is that the likeliest candidates are spermicides like nonoxynol-9 and octoxynol, and they have a tendency to irritate a woman's vaginal lining – thus increasing her risk of infection.

But the government needs to devote far more resources to the fight for a cure. And the occupant of the White House as I write this, George Bush, has not provided very encouraging leadership. He recently stated that AIDS 'is a disease that can be controlled for the most part by individual behaviour. I don't think passing out condoms is the way you affect individual behaviour.' In the fall of 1991, the Bush administration blocked a comprehensive survey of adolescent sexual practices – a survey that would have provided vital information in the fight against AIDS and other sexually transmitted diseases – after critics charged that its questions about oral and anal sex were too explicit.

Mr. Bush is certainly entitled to his traditional values and his squeamishness about explicit materials. I feel the same way myself sometimes. Unfortunately, it's a little too late for his kind of approach to accomplish what needs to be accomplished. What we do know about teenage sexual activity suggests that it's so widespread that any attempt to change this 'individual behaviour' would not put a dent in the HIV epidemic. Most teenagers don't know anyone their own age with AIDS – in large part because the disease has such a long incubation period – so they think they are invincible. How wrong they are. In recent years, approximately one-fifth of the people infected with HIV have been teenagers, and the number is doubling every year.

The really chilling news is that the example and educational efforts of Magic Johnson may not have a long-term affect on this group. A few months after his announcement, high-achieving high-school seniors were polled nationwide. Of those who said they were sexually active, 42 percent said they would continue to have sexual intercourse even if a condom were not available, and 12 percent said they never used a condom – 4 per cent *more* than in a similar poll taken before the Johnson announcement.

The news among college students isn't any better. A survey of California collegians reported in *Newsweek* in December 1991, found that less than 20 percent of the sexually active women used a condom three-quarters of the time or more. A survey of Canadian students, published in the Journal of the American Medical Association in June 1990, was even more depressing. Among highly sexually active individuals (those having had ten or more partners), only 21 percent of the men and 7.5 percent of the women reported regular condom use.

It's clear that a substantial case of denial is still in force in the heterosexual community. What's even more alarming is that gay men, whose response to the crisis was initially so admirable, have begun to backslide. Two recent studies in San Francisco found, respectively, that 16 and 19 percent of gay men who had previously practised safer sex had reverted to high-risk behaviour.

This is understandable, for two reasons. First, while it may be relatively easy to make resolutions about changing behaviour in the first stages of a crisis, it gets a good deal harder as year after year passes by. It's like someone who never wears a seat belt and escapes unharmed from an auto accident. You can be sure that this person will buckle up every time he or she gets in the car – for a week, for a month, for a year. But for five or ten years? That's another story. And think how much more inconvenient *always* wearing a condom is compared to buckling a seat belt.

Second, new medications and treatments are making it possible for people with HIV and even AIDS to stay healthier and live longer, giving a false sense of security that may promote relapses into risky sex. In fact, there is a chance that the longer a person survives with HIV the *more* likely he is to pass it on to a sex partner.

Equally troubling are the indications that

younger gay men have not heeded the safer-sex call as well as their older counterparts. Another 1990 San Francisco study, reported in *Society*, found that 41 percent of a random sample of gay and bisexual men aged twenty to twenty-four were HIV-positive, suggesting that they engaged in high-risk sex in the mid-1980s, precisely the moment when the safer-sex message was being sent out loudest and clearest in the gay community.

No, the news, for the most part, isn't good. That's why it's so important that you, the person reading this book, develop as full an understanding as possible of, first, the risks (if any) you're currently under and, second, the best, sexiest, and most pleasurable ways to reduce them.

Read on.

CHAPTER II

Safer Sex – The Basics

A SUREFIRE WAY TO AVOID HIV, AIDS, AND OTHER SEXUALLY TRANSMITTED DISEASE (AND PREGNANCY, TOO)

Abstinence.

That probably isn't what you want to hear. The fact remains that there are only two foolproof ways to make sure you don't contract HIV sexually. The first is not to engage in sexual intercourse or oral sex. This may or may not be an option for you, but you should be aware of it in any case.

While you're thinking about it, let me waste no time in saying that there are many more kinds of sex than the risky ones. The varieties and pleasures of the (safer) sexual experience is the subject of Chapter IV, but let me say now that dry kissing, caressing, mutual or individual masturbation, sensuous massage, phone sex, vibrators and other sex toys, and body-to-body rubbing are all perfectly safe (as long as certain guidelines are followed) and can all be *extremely* sexy.

The second way to avoid HIV is not to have sex with anyone except a partner who you know, first, is not having sex with anyone *else* and, second, is not infected with HIV.

Both parts of that equation are a little trickier than they might sound, for reasons I'll get to shortly. Suffice it to say that when it comes to fidelity and HIV status, the truth can be hard to come by.

As long as I'm passing out basic information, let me bring up the most important safer-sex tool, a little item called the condom (a.k.a. the rubber, the prophylactic, the raincoat, and, I'm sure, dozens of nicknames I've never heard), to be explored in greater depth in Chapter III. While the use of condoms during sexual intercourse and oral sex does not eliminate the risk of sexually contracting HIV, it greatly reduces the danger, and anyone the slightest bit unsure of a sexual partner's HIV status should *always* use a condom.

A SAFER-SEX GAME PLAN

I feel very strongly that all individuals who are sexually active should devote considered thought to their own and their partner's (or partners') risk of contracting HIV. The first issue to confront is your own HIV status.

You may already be aware of whether you are HIV-negative (meaning that you have not been infected with the virus) or HIV-positive (meaning that you have been infected). You can be almost completely sure you're HIV-positive in one way only:

● You have an antibody blood test for HIV with a positive result.

You can be almost completely sure you're HIV-negative in any of three ways

● You have an antibody blood test for HIV with a negative result – *and*, in the period spanning six months before the test until the present, you have not engaged in oral sex or anal or genital intercourse, or used intravenous drugs;
● You have *never* engaged in any of these high-risk behaviours;
or
● You have *never* used IV drugs and have had sex only with a partner or partners whom you know to be HIV-negative.

ANTIBODY TESTING

If you do know your HIV status, you may skip this and the following sections. Everyone else has a choice to make. Do you get tested or do you not?

Let me delay that hypothetical decision by describing the nature of HIV testing. All HIV tests are what is known as 'antibody' blood tests. They indicate whether the blood contains antibodies (proteins manufactured by the immune system to ward off unwanted foreign material) specific to the HIV virus.

The first test given is called ELISA (for enzyme-linked immunosorbent assay). It is a very accurate test, but it does make mistakes. Specifically, it has a 'false positive' rate of about 2 percent – meaning that out of every hundred times it gives a 'positive' result, that result is incorrect twice. (The rate is even higher in groups with a low incidence of infection.) That's why a second ELISA test is always performed if a blood sample tests positive. If a second test is also positive, then an even more accurate test, usually the Western blot, is performed. If that test shows positive as well, the chances are less than 5 in 100,000 that a mistake has been made. If there is still some doubt about the validity of the test results, still other tests can be taken.

The ELISA test is also capable of giving

'false negative' results (although the rate for these is less than one percent), which is one reason why many experts recommend that sexually active people always practise safer sex, regardless of the results of their antibody tests.

Timing is important in all things, but it's critical in the matter of HIV-antibody testing. In most cases, antibodies develop within a few weeks of infection, but it can take six months or more for antibodies to appear. In other words, a person can have an 'accurate' negative test result and still be infected.

So, if you have had any *possible* exposure to HIV, the only way to be sure you were not infected is to wait at least six months after the potential infection, and then take the test. If the result is negative, then you are not infected with the virus and you cannot infect others.

If you're involved in a mutually monoga-mous sexual relationship and there is a chance that you or your partner were infected in the past, you both must be tested twice, at intervals of six months (and only engaging in safer sex during the interim), if you want to be certain of your respective HIV status.

If both tests come up negative each time, then you and your partner are free, as far as HIV is concerned, to have any kind of sex you want – safe, safer, or *unprotected*, as long as both of you remain monogamous (and as long as you don't use intravenous drugs). I hate to be a party-pooper, but I must add one caveat. Getting in the *habit* of unprotected sex, even though it poses no risk in these circumstances, may make it more difficult to adopt safer-sex practices if the relationship ever ends. You may, in other words, want to make safer sex a lifelong habit that you don't even have to *think* about.

TO TEST OR NOT TO TEST?

Back to the $64,000 question. Unfortunately, no one can answer it except the person himself or herself. However, the current consensus of medical opinion is that testing is advisable for persons considered at risk of being HIV-infected – people who have engaged in high-risk behaviour or are in high-risk groups, and anyone who has had sexual relations with those people.

There are two good reasons for this, and they both make good sense. The first is that medical treatment is now available to delay, and possibly prevent, the progression of HIV to AIDS, and the earlier in the course of the infection the treatment is begun, the better.

Second, if you are HIV-positive, you put all of your sexual partners at risk. Knowing that this is the case will theoretically make a person more responsible and vigilant in the matter of safer sex than he or she would otherwise have been.

If you are at low risk for HIV, being tested may not be such a good idea. First of all, the possibility of a false positive result exists – carrying with it an unbelievable amount of needless emotional stress.

Moreover, a negative result may give people a false sense of security, making them feel that they are somehow *immune* to HIV, or that it's all right to engage in unsafe sex.

For counselling about whether to be tested, call your National AIDS hotline.

A FEW WORDS ABOUT CONFIDENTIALITY

I was born in Frankfurt, Germany, in 1928. I am Jewish. From those two facts you will probably be able to understand that I am very, very sensitive to issues of privacy and its invasion. That's why I would never advocate mandatory testing for HIV – by the government, by employers, or by anyone else.

I always say this during lectures, and when I do, I can see dozens of heads nodding in agreement, so I have the sense that the consensus of public opinion feels the same way.

Moreover, I believe that anyone who makes the personal decision to be tested for HIV should make every effort to ensure that the results of that test remain absolutely confidential. One way to accomplish this is to use a centre that offers anonymous testing. For help in finding the one nearest you, contact your national AIDS hotline. In the U.S. the Federal Centers for Disease fund alternate test sites (ATSs) where you are assigned a code that identifies your blood specimen without revealing your identity.

Once you have the results, you should be very careful about whom you share them with. If you are HIV-positive, your first step is to see a physician who is experienced in and knowledgeable about the treatment of HIV and AIDS, so that he or she can offer you treatment that will show or stop the disease's progression. No one else needs to know – and since there is proof positive that people infected with HIV are discriminated against, no one should be told unless you have a good reason for doing so. Since HIV infection cannot be transmitted by casual contact, there is no medical reason for your employer, co-workers, or acquaintances to be informed.

If you have a negative result, you may want to keep that confidential as well, asking your physician, for example, if the result can be kept out of your medical records. The reason for this is that some insurance companies take great pains to avoid offering life or medical policies to anyone they perceive to be at risk for HIV infection, a category that in the view of some companies includes anyone who's been *tested*, even if the result is negative.

In some countries the government and some private employers now require antibody testing on the part of all potential employees. In the U.S., if you are applying for a job with the government or one of these firms, it may be advisable to have yourself tested, privately and anonymously, beforehand. That way, you can withdraw your application if you test positive, thus making sure that your infection won't become part of official government records or be known by people who have no right to the information.

RISK REDUCTION

You've probably all heard the following piece of conventional wisdom: When you sleep with someone, you're having sex with everyone *they've* ever been with. Well, it may be conventional, but it's also wise.

My husband and my son are the mathematicians in the family, but I figured this out by myself. Say you sleep with ten people in the course of a year, and those partners themselves have had an average of ten (different) partners a year for the past ten years, and say you know nothing about the HIV status of any of these people. Well, you've exposed yourself to one thousand different people during the year.

Say you have sex with five people with the same hypothetical sexual history: you've exposed yourself to five hundred people. In other words, by limiting the number of sexual partners, you've cut your risk of contracting HIV in half.

And, finally, let's say you have only had sex this year with one person, who in turn has had only four partners over the last decade. Well, you are only exposed to those five people, and your risk is two hundred times smaller than it was in the first example.

The moral of my little exercise is clear: a little selectivity can go a long way toward reducing your chances of contracting HIV (or any sexually transmitted disease).

Depending on where you live, the need for selectivity becomes even more pressing. In many countries AIDS rates vary widely from city to city and from area to area; in some areas, it is extremely unlikely that you would come into contact with an HIV-positive person, while in others it is very possible.

TALKING IT OVER

Selectivity isn't just a numbers game, of course. You can also substantially reduce your risk if you exercise discretion in choosing your partners. From what I've already said, it should be clear that (assuming you don't know the HIV status of a partner) you run the highest risk of contracting the disease if you know the person to:

- Be a male homosexual or bisexual;
- Be an intravenous drug user;
- Be a native of sub-Saharan Africa or of one of the Caribbean countries in which HIV rates are highest;
or
- Have had sexual contact, homosexual or heterosexual, with one or more people in the first three categories.

There are other risk categories as well: prostitutes (and people who have patronised them), crack users, people with other sexually transmitted diseases, and people who have had heterosexual sex with a high number of partners over the past ten years.

If a prospective sexual partner is in one of these high-risk categories, you should either not have sex with that person or be absolutely certain that you follow safer-sex guidelines with him or her.

And how do you find out about prospective partners' pasts? Not necessarily by looking at them. (An HIV-positive person can seem to be the very model of good health.) Not necessarily by drawing conclusions about them. (A construction worker could have engaged in 300 episodes of unprotected anal sex in a year's period; a college professor could use IV drugs.) You find out about them by *talking* with them. We've reached a sorry state in our sexual affairs if it isn't obvious to *everyone* that it's better to talk, to find out about someone, to reach a certain level of intimacy, before having sex. But it's not obvious, alas, so I have to say it.

The time to talk about each other's sexual histories, and about the issue of safer sex generally, is definitely not in the heat of passion. There's an old Hebrew expression: When the penis stands up, the brain goes for a walk. In moments of intimacy, resolutions are forgotten, exceptions made, concerns overlooked, with potentially disastrous results.

No, these things have to be talked about beforehand. But when? It's *hard* to discuss sex with anyone, let alone someone you may have been dating for only a few weeks. You may worry that when you bring the subject up, the other person will say (or think) something like:

'What makes you think I'm interested in having sex with *you*?'

'How dare you imply that I've slept around!' (or 'How dare you imply that I'm gay!')

'If you're asking questions like that, you must be some kind of a slut yourself.'

These fears are real and legitimate, and it's a real possibility that your boyfriend or girlfriend will respond in one of these ways. But the embarrassment is insignificantly minor compared to the death sentence of AIDS. And consider this: if you really think that bringing up the subject of AIDS and HIV would rock the boat of your relationship, and if your partner utters one of the above statements or something equally obnoxious, it's a good bet that the relationship was headed for trouble anyway.

Obviously, a good deal of discretion and tact is called for. You don't want to show up at your new friend's apartment for your third date with a clipboard, a pencil, a long list of clinical questions, and a demand that he or she provide a notarised copy of the results of a recent HIV antibody test. On the other hand, it's essential that you find out certain things. Bernie Zilbergeld, the author of *Male Sexuality*, and Lonnie Barbach, who has written a number of books on female sexuality, have jointly produced an audiocassette that suggests several nonthreatening, somewhat indirect, and (relatively) painless ways of introducing this difficult but critically important subject.

> You: 'So, what do you think about all this AIDS business?'
>
> Your partner: 'I don't know what to think. Sometimes I think the only answer is celibacy.'
>
> You: 'Well, I haven't gone that far yet, but I don't have sex with anyone anymore till I've got to know them, and then I always use condoms. How about you?'

Here's another one:

> You: 'Do you think it's true what the media have been saying about AIDS. Do you think everyone is at risk?'
>
> Your partner: 'I don't know what to think. The media have a way of blowing things out of proportion. But on the other hand, sex today can involve real risks. So I play it safe.'
>
> You: 'Yeah, how?'
>
> Your partner: 'I'm more cautious than I used to be. I make sure I get to know people before I go to bed with them. And I always use condoms.'

Let me remind you, finally, that bringing up the subject of safe sex means you are interested

in a person sexually. And that itself can be very
sexy. Use your imagination.

SEX, LIES, AND HIV

Now that I've praised talking to the skies, I
have to add a caveat: talk is cheap.

Talking about AIDS is so difficult that some
people feel that merely bringing up the topic
satisfies all their responsibilities. Uh-uh. If you
and your partner have a frank, earnest, and
uninhibited discussion about AIDS (but don't
ascertain that you are both HIV-negative) and
then go ahead and engage in unsafe sex, you
might as well not have said a word.

And let's say someone tells you they aren't in
a high-risk group, or even that they have tested
negative for HIV and haven't engaged in any
risky behaviour since the test. This brings up
the matter of truthfulness and trust, and a
ticklish matter it is. You should be very, very
wary about believing someone who tells you
they can't give you AIDS. I say this not because
of my own cynicism about human nature, but
because there's proof in black and white.
Consider:

● In a survey of HIV-infected men at a Los
Angeles clinic, 45 per cent remained sexually

active after they learned of their infection, and 52 per cent of these *admitted* that they did not reveal their condition to their partners. (Presumably, the actual percentage is considerably higher.)

● In a survey of Southern California college students, 20 percent of the men and 4 percent of the women admitted they would lie about AIDS tests results in order to have sex. Forty-seven percent of the men and 42 percent of the women said they would understate the number of previous sex partners.

These studies merely bolster a conviction that I already had: if you have any doubt at all about a partner's HIV status, you should always engage in safer sex. That way you don't have to worry about whether he or she is telling the truth, whether he or she (or you) received a false negative result on an antibody test, whether or not he or she is a legitimate member of a high-risk group. Best of all, you don't have to worry about worrying.

The cornerstone of a safer sex life, as I said at the beginning of this chapter, is the condom. To find out everything you ever wanted to know about it, turn the page.

CHAPTER III

Condom Nation

Q: I am worried about contracting a venereal disease during sex. What should I do? Also, I suffer from premature ejaculation. Any suggestions? And finally, I would like to increase the size of my penis. What do you recommend?

A: 1. Wear a condom. 2. Wear two condoms. 3. Wear three condoms.
– *Playboy* magazine

While I was writing this book, I went to a U2 concert one night with about 17,000 young people. Strolling the corridors during intermission, I came upon a souvenir stand and was shocked – and delighted – to find that one of the items for sale was a package of two condoms adorned with U2's logo. Naturally, I bought one. A few nights later, I was a guest on a television chat show. On the air, I presented the host with the package, saying he should keep both condoms – I knew just one wouldn't be enough for a man like him. (That brought down the house.)

The point of the story is that condoms, the most important tool in the enterprise of safer sex, are finally beginning to be accepted as a topic of conversation in polite society. I stress the word *beginning*. Although there are an estimated 9,000 scenes of suggested sexual intercourse on television very year, no one on TV ever seems to use a condom (or, in fact, to give any thought at all to contraception or disease prevention). The omission makes the fact that the television networks and most independent stations still won't run condom commercials even more shameful. In movies, too, people usually just jump into bed as if there were no conceivable consequences. And the uproar with which some people greeted New York and other cities' plans to distribute condoms in the schools demonstrated that for them condoms are somehow secret and dirty.

Still, the days when you have to furtively whisper your request to a pharmacist for a condom are over. They're on display and freely available in just about every drugstore and supermarket, and there are new condom boutiques in New York, Los Angeles, San Francisco, and Philadelphia. In a four-star hotel in Montreal, condoms are in the basket of toiletries provided for all guests. The city of Cambridge, Massachusetts, recently passed an ordinance requiring that all restaurants have condom vending machines in rest rooms for both sexes. A young friend of mine recently went to a college party where there was a big bowl of condoms on a table, free for the taking, where mixed nuts or M & M's might once have been. A definite sign of progress – and condoms don't have any fat or cholesterol!

'THE ENGLISH RIDING COAT': A BRIEF HISTORY OF CONDOMS

Surprise! There actually was a Doctor Condom – or so the story goes. He was supposed to have been the court physician to Charles II of England in the seventeenth century, and to have fashioned a primitive implement out of sheep's intestines scented with perfume. But in fact, the Italian anatomist Fallopius (identifier and namesake of the Fallopian tubes) had created a condom a hundred years earlier. It was made of linen, and Fallopius contended that of the eleven hundred men who used it in his experiment, not one was infected with venereal disease. Among its advantages, he said, was that it could be carried in a trouser pocket.

Another advantage became recognised as condoms (spelled in a variety of ways and also known as 'machines') gained wider currency in the seventeenth and eighteenth centuries; besides being a prophylactic against disease, they were an effective means of contraception. This was appreciated by the English poet White Kennett, who in 1724 wrote a delicious ode in praise of the condom, entitled 'The Machine, or Love's Preservative':

Hear and attend; In CUNDUM's praise
I sing and thou, O Venus! aid my Lays
By this machine secure, the willing Maid
Can taste Love's Joys, nor is she more afraid
Her swelling body should, or squalling Brat
Betray the luscious Pastime she has been at.

The man who really put condoms on the literary map was the eighteenth-century Italian libertine Casanova. He was extremely attached to them, which is evident from the number of affectionate nicknames and descriptions he came up with: 'the English riding coat'; 'the English vestment which puts one's mind at rest'; 'the preservative sheath'; 'assurance caps'; and 'preservatives that the English have invented to put the fair sex under shelter from all fear'.

The condom once failed Casanova. As is so often the case in the present day, it was a result of human factors, not faulty construction. 'The girl came back with the packet of twelve condoms,' he wrote in his autobiography, referring to one of his legion of conquests. 'I put myself in the right position, and ordered her to choose one that fitted well. "This one doesn't fit well," I told her. "Try another." Another, and another, and suddenly I splashed her well and truly.'

The first condom tycoon was apparently one Mrs. Philips, a late-eighteenth-century London vendor who, she boasted in a handbill, 'has had *thirty-five years experience*, in the business of making and selling machines, commonly called implements of safety, which secures the health of her customers'... The following lines are very applicable to her goods:

To guard yourself from shame or fear,
Votaries to Venus, hasten here;
None in my wares e'er found a flaw,
Self preservation's nature's law.

Unfortunately, early condoms were notoriously inefficient. Not only are animal intestines potentially permeable by the bacteria that cause gonorrhea and other sexually transmitted diseases, but the condoms were not particularly well-secured, being tied to the base of the penis by a ribbon. In his *Treatise of the Venereal Disease*, translated into English in 1737, Jean Astruc fumed, 'They ought to arm their penis with oak, guarded with triple plate of brass, instead of trusting to a simple bladder, who are fond of committing a part so capable of receiving infection to the filthy gulph of a harlot.'

The extreme disgust in evidence in this quotation (which, like the Kennett poem, was unearthed by Ronald O. Valdiserri, M.D.) is evidence that objections to condoms have *always* had more to do with the moral views of those doing the objecting than with anything else.

Nonetheless, by the 1800s, this condom recipe was found in many home remedy books. 1. Take the intestines of a sheep and soak in water. 2. Turn inside out and then soak in a weak alkaline solution. 3. Scrape and then disinfect with vapour from burning brimstone. 4. Wash, blow up, and dry. 5. Cut to proper length and tie with ribbon at end.

My readers are invited to try this for themselves. I cannot, however, guarantee the results.

Possibly the most important milestone in the history of the condom took place in 1843, when the process of vulcanising rubber was discovered. Now, for the first time, inexpensive, effective rubber condoms could be mass-produced. (And now the condom had a new nickname.) The next, and final, advance in condom technology came in the early 1930s, when they began to be made of latex, a rubber product that could be made thinner and stronger than the traditional crepe rubber.

But the improvement of the condom mattered little to moralistic guardians of virtue, who have always been outraged by the prospect of its widespread use. The Comstock Act, passed by Congress in 1873, outlawed the dissemination of 'obscene' publications and put forth a definition of obscenity that included information pertaining to the 'prevention of pregnancy'. So writing about condoms was a crime. Not even World War II – in which every G.I. was offered condoms, lectured about their importance, and sent off to battle with the slogan, 'If you can't say no, take a pro' – could change the perception of the product as unfit for polite conversation. (A new use for condoms was discovered as a result of the war, however. During the amphibious landing at Dunkirk in 1942, Allied troops were told to cover their rifle barrels with rubbers.)

The condom fell into further disrepute in the 1950s and '60s, as a result of two factors. First, penicillin and other antibiotics were found to be an effective treatment against syphilis and gonorrhea, thus lessening the perceived importance of preventing infection. And second, the widespread use of birth-control pills was an effortless and risk-free way (or so it seemed) of dealing with the issue of contraception.

Interestingly, condoms became much more respectable in other countries – particularly in Europe and the Far East – than in the United States. One more way that Japan is ahead of us is that a full 43 percent of married couples report using them (the figure here is 10 percent), and there's a condom vending machine on many street corners. When I visited China recently, I was pleased to discover a bowl full of condoms, free for the taking, in every drugstore.

In America, it was not until the magnitude of the AIDS epidemic began to be understood in the early and mid-1980s that 'the English riding coat' began to shed its sordid image. Condom ads (for some reason they almost always featured couples taking moonlit walks on the beach) began to show up in newspapers and magazines; in 1985, I personally made the first condom commercial for cable TV. (I insisted that all crew members take home samples.) Condoms were featured – as a normal part of sexual relations – in movies like *Broadcast News*, *Dragnet*, *Mystic Pizza*, and *Two Moon Junction*. They were even discussed – gasp! – in such TV shows as 'Cagney and Lacey', 'Valerie', 'Kate and Allie', and 'Days of Our Lives'.

But the biggest milestone was the Surgeon General C. Everett Koop's 1986 report on AIDS. In black and white, he declared that if abstinence and mutual monogamy with an uninfected mate were not options, then 'a rubber (condom) should always be used during (start to finish) sexual intercourse (vagina or rectum).' The condom was finally a respectable member of society.

Today condoms are recognised as, first, a contraceptive option that combines exceptional effectiveness with negligible side effects and, second, absolutely the only preventive measure that can be taken by sexually active people who want to continue to have intercourse. Casanova would have been proud.

DO CONDOMS WORK?

Absolutely.

A study presented at the Sixth International Conference on AIDS, held in San Francisco in 1990, observed two sets of couples in which one member was HIV-positive, the other HIV-negative, over a year's time. Of the eighty-nine couples who used condoms irregularly or not at all in their sexual intercourse, there were nine cases in which the HIV-negative partner was infected. Eighty-eight couples used condoms regularly. In not one case did the HIV-negative partner become HIV-positive.

Having said that, I must add that using condoms doesn't *guarantee* that you will not be infected by HIV during sex. In explaining why this is so, I'll begin with something that seems obvious to me, but needs repeating anyway. Some people 'use condoms' – but not all the time. Sometimes they don't have one with them; sometimes they're carried away in 'the heat of the moment'; sometimes they give in to a partner's insistence on unprotected sex; sometimes they just forget. These folk are fooling themselves. With condom use – as with birth control – sometimes just doesn't cut it.

It is possible, too, for condoms to fail (although the majority of condom failures are the result of improper use rather than mechanical failure).

One thing you don't have to worry about is the possibility of the HIV virus passing *through* an intact latex condom. Numerous studies have confirmed this, my favourite being one published in the August *Journal of the American Medical Association*. The HIV virus was placed inside a series of condoms and then, the authors wrote, 'Each condom was mounted on a hollow dildo and placed in a glass cylinder... Intercourse was simulated by pumping the dildo up and down in the cylinder.' The result: none of the condoms leaked. And I can only imagine what fun the researchers had doing the experiment.

There is, however, a possibility that HIV can pass through a *non*-latex condom. Approximately 5 percent of the condoms sold in the United States are referred to as 'lambskin' or 'natural'. (They're actually made from a sheep's large intestine.) While many men feel that these condoms provide increased sensation, and while they are effective as a contraceptive, their surfaces contain holes that are microscopic but still large enough for the hepatitis B and possibly the HIV virus to pass through. The federal Food and Drug Administration has required the makers of lambskin condoms to include labelling on their packages to the effect that the product is not an effective preventative for the transmission of diseases.

It is also possible, though unlikely, for your latex condom to be defective. Since 1987, FDA inspectors have periodically shown up unannounced at all condom factories to perform tests. They fill condoms with about ten ounces of water, and if pinholes cause leaks in the equivalent of more than four condoms per thousand in any production run, the entire lot must be destroyed. The same test is performed on imported condoms.

What about breakage? It can happen. A recent American study found that in 202 episodes of intercourse using the popular

Trojan-Enz condom, the condom broke in four cases – a failure rate of 2 percent.

One way of minimising the risk of breakage is to consult consumer reports on condoms. In America, the magazine *Consumer Reports* tested the relative strength of forty different condom brands in 1989 by blowing them up with air and seeing how much pressure and volume they could withstand before bursting. All but eight of the tested brands performed well. Obviously it makes sense to steer clear of the poor performers, even if they are cheaper.

A final, and more serious, condom pitfall is slippage. The same study that found a 2 percent breakage rate reported that 13.6 percent of the time, the condom slipped off either during intercourse or withdrawal.

One way of minimising the risk of condom failure is the use of spermicides. Nonoxynol-9, the active ingredient in most over-the-counter spermicides, has been shown to kill the HIV virus in laboratory tests, and some prelubricated condoms include the substance in their lubricant. (This is clearly marked on the label.) Researchers aren't certain if it can be just as lethal outside the lab, but I would still recommend taking the extra precaution of putting some additional spermicide – available in drugstores in foam, gel, or cream form – in the tip of the condom, and also applying it to the anus or vagina. (Additional spermicide should also be applied if your condom happens to break.) The nonoxynol-9 in spermicides varies in concentration from 1 percent to 12 percent; if you or your partner finds that the first one tried is irritating, switch to a product with a lower concentration.

HOW TO USE A CONDOM

In most cases, slippage and other condom failures are not the condom's fault – they are the user's. For example, if the condom is not unrolled all the way to the base of the penis when it is put on, slippage during intercourse becomes more likely. And if the rim of the condom is not held against the base of the penis during withdrawal, slippage becomes *much* more likely.

Unfortunately, a lot of people don't know the proper way to use a condom. It's not brain surgery, but the fact is that it's not taught in school and parents are often embarrassed to give this kind of instruction to their children. So, like sex, condom use generally becomes a matter of trial and error. Trying and erring with sex is fun; but as far as condoms go, it's playing with fire.

I have one word for people who haven't used condoms before – practise. This gets them familiar with the shape and feel of rubbers and lets them avoid at least one quite common mistake – using them inside out. Do it with your eyes open and closed. Men can use themselves as guinea pigs, of course. I usually recommend that women use inanimate objects; bananas and cucumbers work nicely. They can do it alone, but practising with a friend can be much more fun.

One word of caution: the intake of drugs and/or alcohol severely impairs small motor skills. In plain language, if you're drunk or high, putting a condom on can be a pain in the posterior. What's more, drugs and alcohol can also affect your judgment, making you more likely to engage in risky behaviour you'd avoid when sober. As a high-school teacher of my son's used to say, a word to the wise is sufficient.

Here's how to use a condom:

● Use a new condom for every act of intercourse and oral sex.
● Put the condom on after the penis is erect and before any contact is made between the penis and any part of the partner's body. *Don't* wait until just before you come. It's possible that pre-ejaculatory fluid may contain the HIV virus.
● Open the package carefully, so as not to damage the contents. Don't bite it or use

scissors or sharp fingernails.

● If the penis is uncircumcised, pull the foreskin back before putting on the condom.

● If using a spermicide, put some inside the tip of the condom.

● Some condoms have a reservoir at the top to hold semen. If yours does not, pinch the tip enough to leave a half-inch space for the semen to collect.

● If your condom does have a reservoir, squeeze all the air out of it.

● While pinching the top of the condom, place it on top of the penis and unroll it all the way to the base. If you accidentally put it on top of your penis upside down, throw it away and take out a new condom. (Pre-ejaculatory fluid may have touched the outside of the condom, and it is possible that this can contain the HIV virus.)

● If you're using lubricant or spermicide, put more on the outside of the condom. More about lubricants later.

● If you feel the condom break during inter-course, stop immediately and withdraw. Do not continue until you put on a new condom.

● After ejaculation and before the penis gets soft, grip the rim of the condom and carefully withdraw.

● To remove the condom, gently pull it off the penis, being careful the semen doesn't spill out.

● Wrap the used condom in a tissue and throw it in the trash. (Don't flush it down the toilet – it

may clog the plumbing.)
• Wash your hands with soap and water.

Most condoms come prelubricated (nonlubricated ones are preferable for oral sex), but many people choose to use additional lubrication. This is an excellent idea – besides increasing comfort, lubricants can reduce the chance that the condom will break. Apply the lubricant generously to the outside of the condom after it has been put on. Use *only* water-based lubricants, such as K-Y Lubricating Jelly. Spermicides also function well as lubricants and don't need to be supplemented with any other product. Oil-based lubricants - mineral oil, baby oil, Vaseline, cold cream, cooking shortenings, and hand creams containing these oils – weaken latex considerably and should never be applied to a condom.

Condoms do not have an unlimited life. They can last five years or so if stored properly; after that they become brittle and much more subject to breaks and tears. When you are about to buy a package, check its expiration date, and don't buy if it has passed (or even if it's a few months away). Don't buy if there's no expiration date, either.

Heat and light can weaken condoms and shorten their life spans, so they should be stored in a cool, dry place – such as a closet or drawer. Your car glove compartment is a no-no. So, alas, is the condom's fabled repository, a guy's wallet. Keeping it there for an evening is okay. Keeping it there all through high school and college means that you will graduate with a worthless rubber.

Some videotapes demonstrate proper condom technique, and give an idea of how they can be made erotic and fun (a subject I'll get to in a minute).

ORAL SEX AND CONDOMS

Unprotected oral sex is considered an unsafe practice. But you can make it safer with condoms. For fellatio, use unlubricated latex condoms, and be sure to put the condom on before there is any mouth-to-penis contact.

Some people like to season their oral sex with flavouring – whipped cream or chocolate syrup, for example. Make sure you don't use anything oil-based, and make sure you put on a new condom before intercourse.

Condoms obviously won't work for cunnilingus or oral-anal sex (sometimes called rimming), but there's a condom substitute. It's called a dental dam, a five-inch square piece of latex designed for use in dental surgery. In America they're available in medical-supply stores and some sex shops. They sometimes come sprinkled with talc, and if so need to be rinsed off first. Whenever there is oral-genital or oral-anal contact, simply make sure the dental dam is always between the mouth and the genitals or anus. Use each dam only once; when you're done, throw it away.

The problem with dental dams, especially if you and your partner like to move around during sex, is making sure they stay put. One possible solution is to fashion a sort of surgical mask out of the dam, holding it in place with elastic ties. Some mail-order suppliers of sex aids sell contraptions that hold dental dams in place.

You might also want to consider the use of surgical gloves during sex. I would recommend them if you have any kind of cuts or rashes on your hand and a) you touch the vagina of a menstruating woman who is (or may be) HIV-infected, or b), you engage in 'fisting', the practice of stimulating the rectum by inserting the fist. Use plenty of spermicide or water-based lubricant, and, needless to say, after using the glove, discard it before putting your fingers in your mouth or any part of your body through which HIV can be transmitted.

WHICH CONDOM DO YOU BUY?

Faced with a drugstore condom display,

some people are overwhelmed with the dizzying choice they have to make. But despite the sheer number of condoms on display, each with its own exotic, usually mystifying brand name, there are really only five basic choices to make: latex versus lambskin; lubricated versus non-lubricated; spermicide versus no spermicide; reservoir end versus plain end; ribbed versus smooth. I've already given my opinion on the first three, but I'll review for those who skipped the previous section. For disease prevention, *always* use a latex condom. And I recommend the use of condoms lubricated with spermicide.

I also recommend reservoir-ended condoms; they eliminate the need to remember to leave a space for the semen yourself. Some condoms are ribbed, the purpose being to provide additional sensation for the partner who isn't wearing it. This is, obviously, a matter of personal choice. The only proviso I would add is that it has been suggested by some researchers that ribbed condoms increase the chance that the vagina or the anus will be irritated, which in turn increases the chance that infection can be spread.

Some condoms are extra thick and may be advisable as a guard against breakage if especially vigorous intercourse or anal sex are anticipated. Finally, although some condoms are labelled 'large', that designation is more for the purchaser's ego than anything else. The fact is that all condoms can stretch as far as you want them to; one size fits all.

Also, be sure that the condom you buy is specifically labelled as providing protection against sexually transmitted disease. Many 'novelty' condoms do not have this designation. They're okay for fun at parties, but they're *not* okay for sex.

Beyond that, I'd recommend trying as many condoms as you can, and seeing which one suits you and your partner best. And that's what I call enjoyable research. It sure beats watching rats run around a maze!

One final point. An estimated 1 to 2 percent of Americans are allergic to latex, the allergy generally taking the form of a rash if their skin is exposed to the substance. You may actually be relieved to know you may be one of these people, having assumed that the irritation on your genitals was the result of a more serious condition. If you think you may be allergic to latex, first have your suspicions confirmed by a doctor. If you are allergic, and you're male, wear two condoms during sex – a lambskin one next to the skin and a latex one over it. If you're female, have your lover wear latex next to the skin and lambskin on top.

FRIENDLY PERSUASION

Believe me, I've heard all the objections to condoms.

- 'Making love with a rubber isn't any fun for me. It's like taking a shower with a raincoat on.'
- 'Groping around in the dark for a condom, opening the package, slopping on the lubricant, putting the thing on – it's too much to do. It interrupts the spontaneity of lovemaking.'
- 'Condoms are icky.'
- 'If I ask my partner to use a condom, it'll make it seem as though I don't trust/love him/her.'
- 'When my partner asks *me* to use a condom, it makes me seem as though he/she doesn't trust/love *me*.'
- 'The whole subject is too embarrassing to talk about.'

Before I deal with these in detail, let me say one thing. Any inconvenience, awkwardness, or slight reduction in sensation condoms might cause is made up for, a thousandfold, by the knowledge of the protection they afford you and your partner.

If you've taken the time and interest to read this book, and you've got this far, I'm not worried about you. I'm sure you understand the importance of consistently using condoms in any sexual relationship in which you're not absolutely sure that both you and your partner are HIV-negative.

And if you're a man, I'm sure I can trust you to use a condom. Let me just add one additional condom benefit that may not have occurred to you. True, condoms somewhat reduce your sensation during sex. But that also has the effect of delaying ejaculation and prolonging lovemaking – a condom advantage cited by nearly half of the men who responded to *Consumer Reports'* readers poll.

If you're a woman or a gay man, you have to concern yourself with your potential partners. The first issue is when to bring up the matter of condoms. As I said in the previous chapter on the subject of HIV status and safer sex generally, the time is not the heat of passion. Nor is it on the first date (unless you have a definite feeling that the first date is going to include sex). No, it's sometime in between, and, unfortunately, I can't tell you exactly when. But I trust you to be able to find a moment when the probability (or at least the strong possibility) of sex is in the air, and when starting to talk about safer sex is not *too* much of a non sequitor. And remember: the fact that you're raising the issue means that you're interested in him sexually. This is a big turn-on. Use it to your advantage.

What do you say? Well, my best advice is to

raise the subject in a nonthreatening, open-ended, somewhat indirect way. In other words, *don't* say. 'Oh, by the way, if we have sex, we're using condoms. Like it or lump it.'

The point is to get the conversation started. You might, for example, try an approach like this: 'You know, I was just reading about how the number of AIDS cases is going down. That must be because people have really started to use condoms, don't you think?'

Or this: 'I heard they might be coming out with a female condom. Do you think it'll ever work?'

Or this: 'Everywhere I go people are talking about AIDS. Do you think it's really as big a danger as everyone says?'

Sometimes, of course, the direct approach is called for. 'I really like you,' you might say, 'and I have a feeling this relationship is going to be something special. That's why I've got to ask you something really important. Do you use condoms?'

Maybe you really can't bring yourself to broach the subject. You might try some nonverbal communication. Buy a condom. Put it in your pocket or some accessible place. At a sexy moment, slip it into your friend's hand and look into his eyes. If he has *any* sexual interest in you, I guarantee that he will find this extremely intriguing and that he will make every effort to try the condom out with you at the earliest possible opportunity. (If he doesn't have any sexual interest in you, at least you found out.)

Or, if humour is a part of your relationship, try leaving a novelty condom on your friend's dresser. (These items are now big business. I recently dropped into Condom Nation, a Philadelphia boutique devoted to you-know-what and walked out with: 'Peter Meter': The Rubber with a Ruler on the Latex'; 'Licks Flavoured Condom'; 'Designer Yuppie Condoms – Made for Young Upwardly Mobile Professional Pr**ks'; 'Birthday Condom – Too Bad It Only Comes Once a Year!'; 'Stealth Condoms', whose package is in the shape of a fighter plane; and the 'World's Biggest Condom', all twenty-four inches of it. I generally don't think condoms are a laughing matter, and many of these items are clearly marked as not being meant to prevent pregnancy or disease. But I'm all for anything that puts the subject of condoms and safer sex on the table.)

If you choose the verbal approach, your partner might say, 'Oh, I always insist on using condoms whenever I have sex.' If so, you've got nothing to worry about.

But what if he makes a face and, for instance, gives you the 'raincoat in the shower line'? Here's a way to deal with it. Find a condom. Take your lover's hand and unroll the condom on his finger. Then gently touch his finger. You could even lick it, or put the finger on a part of your body (use your imagination). Ask him, 'Could you feel that?' Unless he's a liar, he'll say, 'Yes.' Then tell him, 'I'm no expert, but my understanding is that a penis is more sensitive than a finger.' You'll have made your point.

Every objection is different (and so is every relationship), but, depending on what your uncooperative lover says, here are some comebacks you might try or adapt.

IF HE SAYS	YOU SAY
'It's like taking a shower with your raincoat on.'	'I know it'll feel a little different at first, but after we use them a few times they'll feel like a second skin. And *I'll* feel so much more relaxed that I can guarantee you'll have a better time.'
'Condoms take the spontaneity out of sex.'	'If we make sure they're close by, and we put them on together, sex can be as wild as ever.'
'They're gross.'	'You want to see gross? I'll show you some pictures of people with sexually

transmitted diseases that will knock your socks off.'

'Just this once.'

'Once is all it takes.'

'I don't have any condoms with me.'

'Guess what? I do.'

'Don't you trust me?'

'Of course I trust you. But a lot of times people have diseases they don't even *know* about. Besides, wouldn't *you* feel more confident with a condom?'

'Don't you love me?'

'I don't think risking our lives has anything to do with love. Protecting myself and you is the kind of love I'm interested in.'

'But AIDS is a gay disease.'

'Tell it to Magic Johnson. The latest statistics show that the fastest-growing HIV-infected group is heterosexuals.'

'I'm a virgin.'	'I'm not.'
'I never use condoms.'	'Oh, okay. By the way, it's my most fertile time of month, I'm not using any birth control, and I can't wait to have a child.'
'I'm not diseased.'	'No, I don't believe I am either, but I'm not sure about the gorilla I made love to yesterday.' (Thanks to Susan Zimet and Victor Goodman, authors of *The Great Cover-up: A Condom Compendium*.)

If you can't get anywhere with *any* of your arguments, you'll have to resort to the ultimatum. In other words, 'No glove, no love.'

And if even that falls on deaf ears, I would advise you to rethink the relationship. You're involved with a man who apparently has no regard for your or his own well-being, or for your feelings on a vitally important subject. Wouldn't you really be better off without him?

NEW DEVELOPMENTS

It may be hard to believe, but after four hundred years, there's still room for improvement in the condom. One thing scientists are working on is a polyurethane model, which could supposedly be half the thickness of latex but twice the strength, would have a longer shelf life, and would not be adversely affected by the use of oil-based lubricants.

But the most exciting development is the prospect of a female 'condom'. In February 1992, the Food and Drug Administration gave provisional approval to such a device, called Reality and marketed by a small Wisconsin pharmaceutical company. It is a loose-fitting polyurethane pouch that a woman can easily slip into her vagina before intercourse. The closed end of the device is anchored inside the vagina with a small plastic ring; the outer, open end also has a ring. In the U.K. a similar device called Femidon, has recently been launched.

The potential advantage of this item is obvious: it would, for the first time, put the power to make sex safer literally in the hands of women, who in heterosexual intercourse are the parties most at risk of contracting HIV.

According to Reality's manufacturer, the pouch is effective both as a contraceptive and as a way of preventing sexually transmitted disease. Of 1,700 couples who used it in an experimental test, 75 percent of the women and 80 percent of the men reported liking it, and it broke or slipped only 3 percent of the time (a number that compares favourably with the failure rate of conventional condoms).

HOW TO STOP WORRYING AND LOVE LATEX

So both of you are convinced of the importance of condoms. What now?

The first step is to experiment with different condoms, and different ways of using them, to find out what suits you best. Try ribbed and not ribbed, lubricated and dry, thick and thin. Some men like to use two condoms (lambskin under latex, perhaps), because they find that the friction created by the two is pleasurable. Others like the sensation they get when they put a drop of lubricant in the tip of the condom.

The next challenge is to eroticise the condom – to make it a sexy mainstay of your love life. In attempting to do so, the first thing to remember is that the most powerful sex organ in the human body is the brain. In other words, if you associate the look, feel, taste, and smell of condoms with great sex, they will become sexy. Take a lesson from all those horny guys in the 1950s – just a glimpse of a rubber was enough to send them into fits of ecstasy.

So *don't* slip the condom on surreptitiously, as if you're ashamed of it. And don't wait till just before the moment of intercourse. Make it part of your foreplay. It can be sexy to watch a man put on a condom, or to stroke his scrotum or the ridge between his anus and penis while he does the honours. It can be even sexier to put it on *for* him, all the while telling him how wonderful his penis is. It's even possible – and extremely erotic – to put the condom on him with your mouth and tongue. (The most important challenge here is to avoid touching his penis with your tongue before the condom is on all the way. Before trying this manoeuvre, I'd suggest extensive practice with a cucumber or banana.)

How about incorporating the condom into your sexual fantasies and playacting? Susan Zimet and Victor Goodman suggest a few quite promising scenarios in their book *The Great Cover-up*:

● She is a fastidious French maid who has to make sure that everything is in its proper place – including the condom.
● She's a salesperson in a condom store who's dedicated to making sure that every customer has a perfect fit.
● He's a doctor who always wears a rubber glove – and it's not on his hand.

But the sexiest thing of all about the condom is the simplest: the proof it offers that you and your partner care about each other, and the thought that it will help you both stay healthy enough to have terrific sex for years to come.

CHAPTER IV

Safer Sex Is Terrific Sex

Let's say you know (or strongly suspect) that your sexual partner is HIV-positive. Let's say you know (or strongly suspect) that *you* are HIV-positive. Let's say you're not willing to take the chance that a condom will break or slip off during sex. Or let's say that, for whatever reason, condoms are not just an option for you.

As the song says, don't worry, be happy.

There are many ways to have a satisfying, stimulating, even safer sex life – so many, in fact, that the only limit is your own imagination. For far too long, we have been told, explicitly and implicitly, that some kind of *penetration* is the only goal of sex, as if it were a form of drilling. A side benefit to the pursuit of safer sex is a chance to rediscover just how varied the delights of the flesh can be.

(VIRTUALLY) SAFE SEX TOGETHER: THE FIRST COURSE

There's a new buzzword in sex circles – 'outer course'. It means, as you've probably already guessed, sex without intercourse. I like it!

If you want to have a sexual relationship with a partner and you want to virtually eliminate the possibility of infection (that is, if you want to avoid *any* contact, between the genitals and the vagina, the rectum or the mouth), let me present you with an outercourse menu. Much of it, you'll notice, is activity that has traditionally been defined as 'foreplay'. In the safer-sex era, foreplay gets the spotlight – not just a preliminary anymore, it can be an end in itself. Anyway, feel free to choose one from Column A, one from Column B, and combine in any way you want.

(Before I start, let me offer a few words of caution. What makes unsafe sex unsafe is exposure to infected bodily fluids, specifically blood or semen. Keep this in mind and take appropriate precautions. If one partner has open wounds or sores of any kind, contact may not be a good idea. If a man is likely to ejaculate during sex play, he may want to wear a condom even in the absence of penetration. If you have cuts or sores on your hands, wear rubber gloves. Also, while all the activities I describe are completely safe, that doesn't mean a hill of beans if you allow yourself to get carried away and follow them up with unsafe sex. So talk about the ground rules beforehand, and don't get carried away.)

For appetisers, let me suggest some everyday activities that can be sexually supercharged. Talking, for example. I'm not referring to Hi-how-are-you-fine-and-you-not-too-bad-what-do-you-think-of-this-weather. No, what I mean is concentrated conversation where each partner says exactly what he or she thinks of the other person, how he or she would go about doing it and what it would feel like. Some people call this 'talking dirty', but if you devote enough time and thought to it, there's not much that's sexier.

Another everyday activity is eating. But anyone who's seen *Tom Jones* knows that it can be a kind of steamy but completely safe sex. Feed your lover a lobster; have her feed you a mango. The sloppier the better. (Just remember to wear a bib.) Once you've mastered this, why not try using your lover as a *plate* and slather him with whipped cream and fresh berries. No spoons allowed – eat your dessert up with your fingers and tongue.

Anthropologists have suggested that dancing originated as a symbolic form of sexual expression, and anyone who has completely let go while doing the tango knows the truth of that. Indeed, one of the sexiest scenes in recent movies was in *Witness*, where the big-city cop played by Harrison Ford wordlessly led Kelly McGillis, as a young Amish woman, around a barn to the music from a car radio. He didn't even kiss her – but the heat in that barn could have cooked a pot of chicken and dumplings. So take your lover out to trip the light fantastic, and see how much heat the two of you can generate.

Smell is probably the most underrated sense, but it might be the sexiest. A woman I know once told me that there's not much she finds more satisfying than to set her husband down on the bed, take off all his clothes, and just sniff him all over. (A word of caution: personal hygiene, always advisable for sex, is especially important in this kind of thing.)

Moving on to sight and sound, I come to the subject of sexy movies. Ever since I saw Rhett Butler kiss Scarlett O'Hara when I was a little girl, I've known that movies can be *extremely sexy*. They're even sexier when you watch in the privacy of your bedroom with a special friend.

Things have got more explicit since the days of *Gone with the Wind*; a recent Hollywood film like *9½ Weeks*, with Kim Basinger and Mickey Rourke, would have been classified as hard-core pornography a few years ago. But there aren't many mainstream movies as sexy as that, so it's fortunate that X-rated movies are no longer the province of stag parties and dirty old men. They are better produced than they used to be, and many of them are no longer marked by the violence, male-centeredness, and disdain for women of days past. Indeed, sexually explicit films are now the third most popular category of videotapes for rental (after new releases and children's films) and, according to recent statistics, 63 percent of them are rented by women or couples.

I'm no X-rated expert, so, if you're interested in getting some guidance on which films to rent or buy, let me give you the list of American 'Classic Erotic Videos' compiled by the Good Vibrations shop in San Francisco.

- *Legends of Porn*. A retrospective of the most famous x-rated performers.
- *The Devil in Miss Jones*. A 1972 classic.
- *Classic Films of Irving Klaw*, Volumes 1 and 2. 1940s bondage flicks that are unintentionally campy today.
- *Only the Best*. A four-volume series of classic scenes from X-rated cinema. Couples will be interested in 'Only the Best Love Scenes for Loving Couples'.
- *The Story of O*.
- *Nightdreams*.
- *Cafe Flesh*.
- *Autobiography of a Flea*.
- *The opening of Misty Beethoven*.
- *Insatiable*. Starring Marilyn Chambers,

whose most famous role was in *Behind the Green Door*.

● *Erotic in Nature*. The first lesbian-made feature.

● *Suburban Dykes*. Also, obviously, lesbian-oriented.

Some of the gay-made-oriented films recommended by Good Vibrations are: *A Few Good Men*, *Pleasure Beach*, *Powertool*, and *Skin Deep*.

THE MAIN COURSE

Now let's move on to the main course. The first selection, frottage, is something that your cat is probably familiar with; the dictionary defines it as 'the practice of getting sexual stimulation and satisfaction by rubbing up against something, esp. another person'. It can be highly gratifying, and, because penetration is not the goal, there are far more conceivable positions than during intercourse. Try them all out. (Many women like to straddle a lover's thigh and move around for all they're worth.)

The most popular variety of frottage is what is vulgarly known as 'dry humping'. It involves simulating intercourse without removing the clothes, and it can be highly satisfying for both men and women.

Two somewhat tricky manoeuvres are what are known as 'interfemoral' and 'intercrural' intercourse. What they mean, respectively, is simulating intercourse by moving the penis back and forth between the thighs or between the calves. (Lubrication is advised for both.) You might also try between the breasts and between the cheeks of the buttocks.

You could write a whole book on sensual massage. In fact, it's been done, numerous times; one that I recommend is *Sensual Massage: An Intimate and Practical Guide to the Art of Touch*, by Nitya Lacroix. I take my hat off to anyone who's gone to the trouble of being an expert massager – it's a huge plus in anyone's sensuality education. (In fact, if the words 'Expert in massage giving' ever appeared in a personal ad, I predict that person's phone would ring off the hook.)

The variations are endless, the learning process never-ending, the possibility for pleasure limitless. What it comes down to, though, is simple: touching your partner's body in a pleasurable way.

For the fine points, I'd advise consulting a book like Lacroix's. But here are a few basic pointers:

● Relax. Take a hot shower or bath first, have a glass of wine. You may even find that your experience is improved if you masturbate first.

● Make the setting as comfortable as you can. The lights should be soft, the television off. Don't just flop on the sofa, but give some thought to the aesthetics of the experience. How about a freshly laundered sheet lined with pillows, on your bed?

● Experiment. Almost anything can constitute massage – caressing your lover's body with a feather, writing the Gettysburg Address on it with your fingers, covering almost every square inch of it with kisses. (Body kisses, incidentally, are great for osculation junkies who don't think openmouthed kissing is safe enough.) Try massage oils, and see which ones have the scent and feel that suit you and your lover. Massage each other in a bubble bath. Do it blindfolded. Stimulate every single part of each other's bodies (except, for the time being, the genitals) to see precisely what feels good.

● Take your time. If you're used to orgasm being the goal of every sexual encounter, that's something you'll have to unlearn for massage. The point here is to go exquisitely slowly, prolonging each moment and sensation.

The ultimate massage, of course, is masturbation. What works for one person works even better for two. You can masturbate yourself as your lover watches, or you can each pleasure each other. Each couple has to work out the dynamics for themselves.

My only advice would be to keep the lines of communication open. This is a sensitive and potentially explosive area. If you feel any embarrassment or discomfort (or you sense that your partner is feeling any), now is not the time to be the strong silent type. Tell what you're feeling; ask what he or she is feeling. If there is a problem, go a little slower, or try a different path. Your sex life and your whole relationship will be the better for it.

A FINAL WORD

'Try pretending that you are a ninth-grader in a parochial school. It is the autumn of 1953. Rubbers are not obtainable and birth control is unheard of.'

These lines (from an article in *People With Aids Coalition Newsline*, by Michael D. Anderson) contain the key to solving one of the main puzzles of safer sex. The puzzle is this: for both individuals and in particular relationships, the main direction of sexual development in our society has always been in one direction. We start with touching ourselves, and proceed to joint activities – holding hands, kissing, petting. The goal is intercourse. Now, however, it behoves us to back *away* from intercourse. How do we unlearn enough of our instincts and social training to do so?

Anderson tells us the way to go. All of us, before we were jaded by time and experience, were capable of intense sexual feelings at a wide variety of provocations: the touch of a hand, a smell or taste that brings to mind a rich memory, the sound of someone's voice, reading a hardly explicit but nonetheless intensely sexy passage in a book, the feel of a silk shirt next to your fingers as you dance a slow dance, the sight of a movie star on a giant screen, a kiss. The challenge is to re-create that state of mind. It may not be easy, but I guarantee you that it can be done.

One technique that works for some people is to create an 'erotic corner' in your home. In a locked drawer or some other special hiding place, put some things that make you feel sexy. It could be erotic paraphernalia like condoms or massage oils; it could be special clothing; it could be a photo of a particular someone.

Whenever you walk by it, think about what's inside. Something will get triggered, a sexually arousing thought. Now, work on using that thought. Store it in your brain, the way a computer does. Soon, even when you're away from home, you'll be able to retrieve that special feeling, and you'll know that you're able to make yourself *feel* sexy, just because you want to be. And when you've mastered that skill, sex can be an integral part of your life, not just a particular bedroom activity.

CHAPTER V

Solo
Flights

You can't give yourself AIDS.

And that's only one of the benefits of masturbation. It can also help make you a better lover, help you learn about yourself, and provide the highest level of sexual pleasure when a partner is unavailable, unwilling or for whatever reason unsuitable.

If it sounds like I'm hyping masturbation, I won't apologise. In Chapter III I talked about all the bad press condoms have got. Masturbation has had it even worse. True, hardly anyone uses the ridiculous term 'self-abuse' anymore, or believes that masturbation will grow hair on your palms, or make you grow crazy or go blind. (I've always loved the story about the teenager who said, 'I'll only do it till I need glasses!') Yet the stigma persists. As recently as 1975, a Vatican pronouncement declared that it was 'an intrinsically and seriously disordered

act'. As open as people have got about every
other aspect of their sex lives, masturbation still
seems to carry with it an element of shame, a
remnant of outmoded religious and moral
restrictions. Many parents have no problem
discussing sexual intercourse with their children, but blush and stammer when masturbation comes up. It's the opposite of the weather:
nearly everyone does it (women as well as men),
but hardly anyone *talks* about it.

One person who did have something to say
about it was Oscar Wilde, who praised it for
being 'cleaner, more efficient, and you meet a
better class of person'. I also like what one of
the respondents to Shere Hite's *Hite Report* had
to say about the pleasures of self-gratification:
'At least I know I'm going to bed with someone
I like.'

Over the past forty years, masturbation has
started to gain acceptance. Probably the biggest
single factor has been the research of the
Institute for Sex Research – more commonly
known as the Kinsey Institute, which showed
how remarkably widespread the practice is.
Even four decades ago, when its research was
conducted, the Institute reported that by age
twenty-five 50 percent of American women and
93 percent of men masturbated. Another
milestone was the publication in 1969 of Philip
Roth's novel *Portnoy's Complaint*. The hero,
Alex Portnoy, was a veritable Jedi Knight of

masturbation – which was good, because at least it brought the topic up in book-review columns and talk shows, but also not so good, because Portnoy was portrayed as, if not deranged, as least extremely kinky. (Who could forget, for example, the image of him masturbating inside a piece of liver? Actually, this is not a bad idea, as long as the meat isn't refrigerated.)

Even more significant has been the development of the craft of sex therapy, of which I am a proud practitioner. Such pioneering sex therapists as William Masters, Virginia Johnson, and Helen Singer Kaplan have long recognised how valuable a tool masturbation can be, of immense aid in an individual's attempt to understand and come to terms with his or her own sexuality. For men, exercises performed during masturbation can be a way of solving the problem of premature ejaculation. And it is perhaps the only way that preorgasmic women can learn to achieve orgasm, first alone and then with a partner.

Another person who deserves credit is Betty Dodson, who for more than twenty years, in books, workshops, and now videos, has spread the word about masturbation. I recommend her book *Sex for One: The Joy of Selfloving* to anyone interested in a sensitive, enthusiastic, and highly personal exploration of the topic.

Ironically, what has made masturbation

more respectable than ever is the spectre of AIDS. For men and women who are concerned about becoming infected with the HIV virus – and for those who already are infected – self-pleasuring is a simple, completely safe, responsible, and potentially very gratifying way to achieve sexual satisfaction.

At this point, we no longer have the luxury of holding on to masturbation myths, stigmas, or taboos. It is a fact of life. If that's hard for some people to swallow, too bad!

CREATIVE MASTURBATION

There's masturbation and there's masturbation. On the one hand (pun definitely intended), the experience can be short, unmemorable, and not-so-sweet – the solo equivalent of wham-bam-thank-you-ma'am. On the other hand, it can be shattering, cataclysmic, and well-nigh earth-moving in its exquisite intensity, endlessly lingering for one delicious moment after another.

Which one would *you* prefer?

This book is not a masturbation manual (to those interested in further guidance, I would recommend picking up a copy of *Sex for One*). But I can offer you some guidelines on how to make the experience as rewarding as possible.

First of all, give some thought to the question of setting. Quickies have their place, but I think most people would agree that their most pleasurable sexual episodes have been richly textured experiences; the more senses that are involved, the better! What goes for sex with a partner, goes for sex with yourself. So don't be surreptitious and furtive when you masturbate. Set aside some time, make sure you won't be disturbed, and make every effort to create the most inviting environment possible. I'm talking candlelight, soft lights, beautiful music – the whole bit. It wouldn't even hurt to put on a sexy outfit.

Second, relax. Meditate, take a long, blissful hot shower or bath, or just sit quietly for a few minutes, let your mind go blank, and listen to your breathing. This is a time when you want to leave the cares and worries of your life behind.

Third, explore your body. Too many people go straight for their genitals. That's like putting the cavalry rescue in the first scene of a cowboys-and-Indians movie! Remember that the largest organ of pleasure on the human body is the skin – there's literally no part of it that doesn't have some erotic potential. Touch yourself all over your body – softly, firmly, with the back of your hand, your fingertips and fingernails. Use a feather; use massage oil. Find out where you're sensitive and where you're not.

Fourth, fantasise. Think back and remember one of your favourite sexual experiences. I'd be willing to bet that it was something other than the intercourse itself that made it so memorable. Was it what your lover was wearing? Was it a special way he or she touched you? Was it the setting (the beach, a deserted office building, a lavish hotel room, the backseat of a Buick)? Was it a nonvisual sensory stimulus – a smell, a taste, a sound? Or was it something else that was going on in your life at the time?

Whatever it was, try to re-create that special feeling. If you relax enough to let yourself go, you will definitely be able to. Try to think about it in slow motion, prolonging the moment of richest anticipation. If you feel your mind racing ahead to the climax, be a good and considerate lover and slow down. Go back to the beginning and play it out again.

For some people, of course, the best fantasies are purely fictional. Let your imagination go wild. Think about a sexy co-worker, a movie star, someone you just glimpsed on the street, or even a completely fabricated creature. You are the writer, director, producer, and star of this movie – take advantage of your power and create the sexiest film possible. Does the idea of watching two people have sex turn you on? Fine. How about sex with a 'forbidden' partner – say, your high-school maths teacher, or maybe the whole high-school football team, singly or together? Again, fine. Or sex, in a 'forbidden' way? No problem – in the world of your imagination, absolutely nothing is forbidden.

Some people like to have help when they fantasise. They like to watch sexually explicit movies, read erotic books, look at sexy pictures. If this appeals to you, got for it! Happily, there has started to emerge a whole new breed of erotica, much of it geared to women, and much less degrading to females than the X-rated stuff of the past. And there are now other places to go for this kind of material than the sleazy sex shop of yore, presided over by a cigar-chomping proprietor. I discussed some of the 'couples' videos in the last chapter, and I'll recommend some books later on in this one.

This kind of imaginative stimulation is so powerful that it's all some people need. One study of easily orgasmic women found that two-thirds of them were able to reach orgasm through fantasy alone, with no need of any bodily stimulation.

Most people, however, find that touching, stroking, or otherwise stimulating their genitals, if not absolutely essential for orgasm, adds to the experience. And here again, experiment. Touch yourself in unusual ways, in different places, at various speeds. Many people (both men and women) find that stimulating the anus during masturbation heightens the sensation;

others strike gold in their nipples or lips or upper thighs. The process, in any case, gives you a completely unpressured environment in which you can find out some important things about your own sexual taste and responses – knowledge you can pass on to your partners when you go back to duo sex in the future.

The experience of orgasm during masturbation encompasses a wide range. For some people, it's more intense than during sex. (Finding this out can let you *incorporate* masturbation into sex, either by your partner or by yourself.) For others it's a calmer, more peaceful sensation. Masturbation guru Betty Dodson has spoken of combining self-pleasuring with meditation, coming up with a unique activity she calls Transcendental Masturbation. By reciting her mantra while masturbating, she wrote, she 'provided natural healing of stresses, changed dis-ease to ease through discharge of sexual energy, and provided a transcendental experience completely in harmony with nature.'

Whatever kind of experience you have – even if its unbelievably transcendental – don't repeat it again and again. The next time you masturbate, try something different. If you're used to lying down, stand up. Do it in a different room of the house, or maybe outside the house – in the backyard under the stars, or perhaps the car. (Don't get *too* carried away while you're driving, and for God's sake don't use two hands.) Wear different clothes, no clothes, or be really kinky and wear your lover's clothes. Try a special hand lotion, or a deliciously scented massage oil. Vary your fantasies.

When you've run through the whole gamut, you'll have a dependable repertoire of scenarios, settings, and techniques. Now, by mixing and matching them at will, you can attempt to create the ultimate experience. You may not get there, but it will sure be fun trying.

JUST FOR MEN

Most men think they're pros when it comes to masturbation. Well, I've got news for you – a lot of you have a lot to learn.

The main problem is that many men learned to masturbate and ejaculate very rapidly. Usually in their early teens, they would get aroused by looking at erotic pictures, having sexy thoughts, or just physical stimulation from their clothing or the way they sat. Because they often didn't have the privacy or time for prolonged masturbation, they would go to the bathroom or under the covers and get it over with as quickly as possible without someone finding them. This behaviour was reinforced for many in army barracks or college dorms, where because of a lack of privacy they had to 'relieve' themselves as quickly and quietly as possible.

A graphic illustration of males' tendency to make masturbation into an Olympic event can be seen in 'circle jerks', where a group of adolescents sit together and masturbate. Who wins the prize? Well, it's *not* the boy who takes the longest time to ejaculate.

Actually, there's an evolutionary reason for this tendency. As Kinsey pointed out, there appears to be an instinctive desire in most male animals to enter the female and ejaculate as soon as possible, because they are at risk from predators during mating.

Even though rapid ejaculation is ingrained this way, it can be unlearned, and without too much difficulty. Here's one way. Once you have an erection, you should put a halt to any fantasies you may have been having and concentrate on the sensations you feel as you stroke your penis. The key is to learn to identify the 'premonitory sensation' – the precise feeling at the 'moment of no return', the point at which ejaculation is inevitable.

After slowly masturbating a few times and concentrating on what it feels like just before ejaculation, you will learn to recognise the feeling just before the premonitory sensation. Then, the next time you masturbate, cease and desist just before the premonitory sensation happens. After a few moments start again, and once more stop at the same place. On the third time, bring yourself to ejaculation.

Now you know that you can delay ejaculation! Congratulate yourself. The next step is to learn how to delay it while continuing to masturbate. The way to learn this step is the same as the way to Carnegie Hall: Practice. If you're a good pupil, you'll be able to control your ejaculations within a few weeks.

This technique has two obvious benefits. First, your own masturbation will be a richer, more prolonged experience. And second, you will become a terrific lover.

Something else that will come as news to many men is that women aren't the only ones who can enjoy masturbating with mechanical assistance. Some men like to do it with a back-of-the-hand vibrator. Others like to use vibrators to stimulate the anus, or, if there's a small, ball-like attachment, the ridge directly under the glans of the penis.

There are also sleevelike vibrators – simulated vaginas, really – that cover the whole penis. You might even want to take a cue from Alex Portnoy. But, please, don't tell the butcher what you're buying the piece of liver for.

JUST FOR WOMEN

For many girls masturbation doesn't come as

naturally or easily as it does for boys. There are many reasons for this – from societal strictures to anatomy – but now isn't the time to go into them. The important point is that women *can* give pleasure to themselves.

You just have to find out what works for you. And try not to be impatient. Some women don't give themselves enough time. If they don't experience sexual arousal and orgasm within ten minutes, they may lose patience, think, *Who needs it*, and give up. My advice is to find some time when you can have at least an hour to yourself, take the phone off the hook, maybe even lock the door. And if it doesn't work, don't lose heart. Wait a few days, and try again. If you're committed to orgasm, I'd be willing to bet that eventually you'll achieve it.

A good way to begin is by lying on a bed, putting your legs up and using a mirror to take a really good look at your own genitalia. Men can *see* theirs; women's are hidden, which may have contributed to the view that what's 'down there' is somehow dirty or bad.

Explore the inner lips and the outer lips and take the time to caress yourself. This may be more comfortable in a bubble bath or a shower. The most intense feelings will come when you begin to stimulate the clitoris. Take the time to explore and discover its need – the speed, rhythm, and force with which it feels good to touch yourself. For some, long, slow, heavy-pressured slides of the finger up and down the clitoris are best. Others prefer short, light flicks back and forth. Still other women like rubbing the clitoris with two fingers spread open on each side.

Some women love to have water directed at the clitoris – from a pulsating shower head, or, if this is physically possible, directly from the tap of the bathtub. Others like squeezing and contracting their thigh muscles while pressing their genitals against a pillow.

You may find that you like to insert something into your vagina or anus while you're stroking the clitoris, like your fingers or a dildo. (To avoid infection, never put a dildo, your finger, or anything else first in your anus and then in your vagina without scrubbing first in soap and water.)

You can even get a dildo at your local supermarket! I quote from the authority, Betty Dodson:

> An organic dildo can be made from a cucumber or zucchini (I have a friend who's crazy about wilted carrots, too). A cucumber can be sculpted to size with a potato parer, but leave enough skin at the bottom for a handle so your lover won't slip away in the night. If you carve too close to the centre seeds, the cucumber will go limp…

One day I was cruising the cucumber bin in a supermarket with such thoughtfulness that a woman standing nearby asked me how I knew which ones were best. 'Mainly intuition,' I said. 'I'm picking out a lover for tonight.' She doubled over with laughter as I winked and walked out.

Another aid to orgasm is the vibrator. For women who have a particularly hard time reaching climax, this machine is the way to go: the vibrations it produces around the clitoris are so strong and steady that the only possible barriers to orgasm are physiological problems or a massive psychological resistance.

There are many different kinds of vibrators available, some that need to be plugged into a wall socket, some battery-operated, some designed for portability. In America you can find them in drug and department stores – where sometimes, for respectability's sake, they are called 'massagers' – or in mail-order catalogues.

Most vibrators fall into one of two basic categories. One resembles a portable electric mixer and includes various attachments to provide different kinds of sensation on the body. The 'wand' type has a cylindrical handle about twelve inches long, with a vibrating knob on the end that looks like a doorknob or a slightly flattened tennis ball.

Perhaps the best vibrators for stimulation of the labia and clitoris is a variant on the wand type called the Eroscillator. Only about seven inches long, it's shaped like an electric toothbrush with an oscillating head and variable-speed motor.

There's another type of vibrator available, but I don't know any women who prefer it. This is the kind, often seen in porno shops, that's shaped like a male penis. It seems to be designed more to reflect male fantasy than to bring pleasure to women.

If you want to know more about the vibrator, there's a whole book on the subject, appropriately titled *Good Vibrations*. (I love the name of the publisher – Down There Press.)

Finally, let me tell you – if you don't already know – about the 'pleasure muscle'. This is the nickname of the pubococcygeus, or 'PC', muscle, the main muscle in the pelvic area. It has a tremendous number of nerve endings, and as a result stimulating it can be intensely pleasurable.

To identify the muscle, lie on your back and place one of your fingers about two inches inside of your vagina. Then contract the muscles in your vaginal area just as if you wanted to stop the flow of urine. You will feel the PC muscle tighten around your finger.

'Kegel exercises' (named for Arnold Kegel, the physician who invented them) strengthen the PC muscle and, for many women, result in more frequent and intense orgasms. To Kegel, simply tighten and relax the PC muscle. (You can do this anywhere, by the way – at the breakfast table, watching TV, or even at a board meeting.) At the start, hold the muscle tight for five or six seconds, then slowly and completely relax it. Do this a dozen times or so, once or twice a day. After a few weeks, you might want to hold the contraction for ten seconds or more.

An added bonus, for some women, is that the exercises are intensely pleasurable in and of themselves. A young woman once told me that she Kegeled while driving to and from work every day. But it felt so good that she was afraid she'd have an accident, so she resolved to do the exercise only when stopped for a red light. Now, whenever she sees another woman stopped at a light, with a look of intense concentration on her face, she smiles to herself and thinks, 'I know what *you're* doing.'

Incidentally, if and when you move on to penetrative sex, the PC muscle can be an important addition to your lovemaking repertoire. If a woman tightens and relaxes the muscle while a man's penis is inside her vagina, the result is a simulated intercourse that (I have been told) can be intensely pleasurable.

FANTASTIC FANTASY

I've already mentioned that the most powerful sex organ in the human body is the brain. Well, sometimes the brain needs a little artificial assistance. The days when those in search of explicit material had to sneak into sleazy porno shops are over. Now the term is 'erotica', and it's found in the best bookstores.

As with masturbation, men have traditionally been more ready than women to indulge in pornography. Most men know whether or not they like it and, if so, exactly what pushes their buttons. Most of them respond to visual stimulation – i.e., the photos in *Playboy* and *Penthouse*. But women are a little more particular, and those interested in going beyond the bodice-ripper genre need a little more guidance. I talked a little about sexy movies in the last chapter; here's a list of some erotic books that you might have fun exploring. (Men are welcome to pick them up, of course. Besides getting turned on, they're likely to learn something about the body female.)

● *The Claiming of Sleeping Beauty*. *Beauty's Punishment*. *Beauty's Release*. All by A. N. Roquelare (a pseudonym for Anne Rice). A sensuous retelling of the story of Sleeping Beauty; heavy on the S/M.
● *Deep Down: The New Sensual Writing By*

Women. The Unmade Bed: Sensual Writing on Married Love. Both edited by Laura Chesler. Two classy compilations.

● *Erotic Interludes: Tales Told by Women. Pleasures: Women Write Erotica.* Both edited by Lonnie Barbach. Two stimulating anthologies, the first composed of fantasies, the second of things that (supposedly) really happened.

● *Erotica: Women's Writing from Sappho to Margaret Atwood.* Edited by Margaret Reynolds. Another literary anthology.

● *My Secret Garden. Forbidden Flowers. Women on Top.* All by Nancy Friday. These groundbreaking books about women's sexual fantasy aren't fiction, but are all the more powerful for it. They've helped countless women discover their *own* secret gardens.

● *Serious Pleasure: Lesbian Erotic Stories and Poetry. More Serious Pleasure.* Both edited by the Sheba Collective. The titles say it all.

● *High Risk: An Anthology of Forbidden Writings.* Edited by Amy Scholder and Ira Silverberg. Behaviour on the edge.

I'd also like to mention a book geared to men – *Hot Living: Erotic Stories About Safer Sex*, edited by John Preston. Sexy doesn't have to mean unsafe, and this anthology proves the point.

Another way to stoke your fantasies is through phone sex, which has become increasingly popular lately. There's even a best-selling (and very sexy) novel about it – *Vox*, by Nicholson Baker.

Phone sex is completely safe – for your body. It could, however, have some bad effects on your bank account. It's not so bad if you have a regular partner; you're only liable for your normal telephone charges. But be wary of commercial sex lines. Their rates, usually charged by the minute, are steep. If it takes you five minutes to masturbate, you could end up footing a hefty phone bill, or becoming a premature ejaculator – and that's something I don't want to see.

The spectre of AIDS may be responsible for the revival of another form of safe sexual fantasy – the topless bar. But where topless bars of yore were smoky dens of iniquity, featuring things like nude mud wrestling, they've now gone upscale, with fifteen-dollar cover charges, valet parking, and, sometimes, topless women who'll type a business letter or send a fax for customers. Some of the bars feature 'lap' or 'couch' dancing, where the dancers strip at extremely close range, ending up in the customer's lap.

You may or may not approve of this kind of thing; I know my feminist friends think it exploits women and perpetuates bad sexual stereotypes. Be that as it may, the clubs have one undeniable advantage: sexually speaking, they're completely safe.

The latest wrinkle in fantasy is 'virtual reality', a computer technology that creates the illusion of immersion in an artificial world. By donning a special mask that essentially has a tiny television screen over each eye, and a glove hooked up to the main computer, you become a full participant in a three-dimensional world that envelops you completely.

So far, this still-developing technology has been used for excursions in science, technology, and design. But there are obviously other applications. Anyone who saw Woody Allen's film *Sleeper* remembers the spherical Orgasmatron – merely laying the hands on it brought one to sexual ecstasy. Well, virtual reality has the potential to take the Orgasmatron several steps further. Listen to how Howard Rheingold describes the possibilities in his book *Virtual Reality*:

'Picture yourself a couple of decades hence, dressing for a hot night in the virtual village. Before you climb into a suitable padded chamber and put on your 3-D glasses, you slip into a lightweight (eventually, one would hope diaphanous) bodysuit, like a body stocking, but with the kind of intimate snugness of a condom. Embedded in the inner surface is a mesh of tiny tactile detectors coupled to vibrators of varying degrees of hardness, hundreds of them per square inch, that can receive and transmit a realistic sense of tactile presence.

'Now, imagine plugging your whole sound–sight–touch telepresence system into the telephone network. You see a lifelike but totally artificial visual representation of your own body, and of your partner's. Depending on what numbers you dial and which passwords you know and what you are willing to pay (or trade or do), you can find one partner, a dozen, a thousand, in various cyberspaces that are no further than a telephone number. You can whisper in your partner's ear, feel your partner's breath on your neck. You can run your cheek over (virtual) satin, and feel the difference when you encounter (virtual) flesh. Or you can gently squeeze something soft and pliable and feel it stiffen under your touch. Six thousand miles away, an array of effectors are triggered, in just the right sequence, at just the right frequency, to convey the touch exactly the way you wish it to be conveyed. If you don't like the way the encounter is going, or your presence is required in physical reality, you can turn it off by flicking a switch and taking off your virtual birthday suit.'

It sure beats going into the bathroom with a copy of *Playboy* and locking the door!

CHAPTER VI

Especially for Women

Let me share some statistics with you. Between February 1991 and January 1992, 5,707 American women were diagnosed as having AIDS. Admittedly, in the scheme of things, this is not a very high number, especially when you consider that in the same twelve-month period, more than 39,000 men were diagnosed with the disease.

So, comparatively speaking, women don't face a very big risk. Right?

Wrong. The 5,707 female AIDS cases represented an 18 percent rise from the previous twelve-month period – nearly three times the rate of increase of male cases. What's more, more than 2,000 of the women – compared to barely 1,000 of the men – got AIDS from heterosexual contact. That's right – more than twice as many women as men currently get AIDS from heterosexual sex.

The figure for women was 22 percent higher than the year before, and proof positive that, especially when it comes to heterosexual transmission, the AIDS threat to women is very large indeed.

Part of the reason for the disparity is simply that more men than women are HIV-infected, and so women are more likely to have an infected heterosexual partner than men are. But it also has to do with the nature of the disease and its transmission. Say Wendy, an uninfected woman, has unprotected intercourse with an infected man. And say Steve, an uninfected man, has unprotected intercourse with an infected woman. You know what? Wendy is far more likely to get HIV than Steve is.

It's not fair. But, then, neither is life.

There are two factors that make women's situations especially perilous. First of all, as I've already mentioned, until a female condom is approved, the ultimate responsibility for practising safer sex is literally in the hands of men. If a guy refuses to wear a condom, no condom is worn. Which is all the more reason for women to take a firm and unshakable 'No glove, no love' position.

I know this kind of obstinence is hard. After all, no one likes to be the bad cop. It would be so much easier just to go along. *It would just be this once, and he seems like such a nice guy*. Then, too, the threat of AIDS has been known for more than ten years. A decade of safer sex may have made you sick and tired of condoms. It may have lulled you into thinking that the danger is over.

I ask you, woman to woman, to try as hard as you can to resist such thoughts. Once is enough. The nicest (and healthiest-looking) guy in the world can be HIV-infected. And the danger is by no means over.

The second factor that women have to be aware of, of course, is that an HIV-positive pregnant woman can pass the infection on to her baby, either during the pregnancy or in childbirth. The infection is transmitted between 30 and 50 percent of the time, depending on how advanced the mother's disease is. (What's more, she has a higher likelihood of developing HIV-related illnesses because pregnancy weakens the immune system.)

Unsafe sex is a double whammy – it can get you sick and it can get you pregnant. So women who know or suspect that a partner is HIV-positive should be doubly certain always to use safer sex practices. Without them, from a single sexual encounter, two people could end up getting a very serious disease.

If you *want* to get pregnant, a host of questions present themselves. Should you get tested for HIV? Should your partner get tested? If he turns out to be HIV-positive, then conceiving a child with him is obviously not a good idea. But what if you are infected? Does that mean you should never get pregnant? If you already are pregnant, should you get an abortion?

These are very, very complex and difficult questions, and should only be resolved after lengthy discussions between women and their doctors and counsellors. If you need some advice on where to go to get advice, start with some of the AIDS hotline numbers listed in the Resource Guide.

Similar considerations apply for women who are considering getting artificially inseminated. If you're using a sperm bank, make sure that it tests its semen and/or donors for HIV, and that it provides pre- and postinsemination counselling for recipients. (And if you were inseminated in the past and don't know the HIV status of the donor, discuss with a doctor or counsellor whether you should be tested now.) If you're supplying your own donor – a friend or a stranger – be just as vigilant in determining his HIV status as you would with a lover. The risk is just the same.

ESPECIALLY FOR LESBIANS

Some lesbians think that AIDS is not their problem. They are sadly mistaken. Substantial numbers of U.S. lesbians have contracted the disease – some through IV drug use, some through atificial insemination from infected semen, some through unsafe sex with infected men (just because a woman defines herself as a lesbian doesn't mean she never has sex with men), but, in at least four cases, from woman-to-woman transmission. (As I've said before, cervical secretions contain HIV and it can be passed during unprotected oral sex.)

So, if you're a lesbian and you're not absolutely sure of the HIV status of yourself and your partner (or partners), please use the safer-sex guidelines I've already outlined. Use a dental dam during oral sex. Consider using well-lubricated (with water-based lubrication) latex surgical gloves if you put your fingers or fist into a partner's vagina or rectum. When using dildos or vibrators, cover the device with a new condom each time it is inserted into a different woman's vagina or rectum. (If no condoms are available, you can scrub the device with a solution of one part household bleach and nine parts water, then rinse with clean water.) And remember that menstrual fluid can contain a high concentration of HIV, so if your partner is menstruating, or you are, be especially vigilant.

CHAPTER VII

Especially for Men

If you're a straight man and you read the statistics in the preceding chapter, showing that women face more of a risk from heterosexual sex than men do, don't be lulled into a false sense of security. Of the American men who were diagnosed with AIDS in the most recent twelve-month period analysed by the Centers for Disease Control, 1,313 got it from straight sex, and a total of 4,803 men have got it that way since the disease was first identified. And thousands and thousands of other straight men are infected with HIV, awaiting (whether they are aware of it or not) the slow but unstoppable time bomb of AIDS. In virtually every case, the disease could have been prevented by the practice of safer sex.

I would normally not single out anyone with the misfortune of having this disease. But, ever since his announcement that he was infected

with HIV, Earvin 'Magic' Johnson has cour-
ageously allowed himself to be a public example
of the need to boost awareness of the HIV/
AIDS situation, so I'll ask you to consider what
happened to him. A heterosexual, one of the
greatest athletes in the world, beloved by nearly
everybody, Magic thought he was invincible.
He was not. And if it could happen to him, it
could happen to anybody.

From the day he made his announcement,
Magic has been clear on one point: *everybody*
who is sexually active should always use
condoms. I will only add, Amen.

I'll give one more reason for men to be
vigilant in their practice of safer sex: the peace
of mind of their partners. You may feel
confident that you're HIV negative, but, if
you haven't been tested at least six months after
your last sexual contact with an HIV-unknown
or HIV-positive partner, you can't be absolutely sure.

And if you're not absolutely sure, insisting,
beseeching, or even requesting that you and a
partner have unprotected sex is putting an
unfair burden on her. On the other hand, letting
her know that you want to use condoms shows
that you care about her and her health. It is one
of the nicest expressions of love I can think of.

ESPECIALLY FOR GAY MEN

If there's any group that understands the dangers and ravages of HIV and AIDS, it is gay men. Nearly every gay man in the country has friends who have died of the disease; some have gone to dozens of funerals. So I'll spare you the lectures.

But I know that many gays – especially young people who weren't sexually active in the mid-'80s, when the disease got the most publicity – don't know all there is to know about safer sex. So allow me to run down some of the basics of safer sex, customised for gay men.

● Unless you and your partner have both been tested negative for HIV and are completely monogamous, always practice safer sex. This is true even if you are both HIV-positive: one partner might have a stronger strain, which could trigger symptoms or the onset of AIDS in the other.

● Anal sex is the single most dangerous practice when it comes to contracting HIV (especially for the recipient). So always use a new latex condom with plenty of water-based lubrication.

● Oral sex is risky. Whenever there is penis-to-mouth contact, always use an unlubricated condom. Put it on as soon as the penis is erect; there is a good chance that pre-ejaculatory fluid ('precum') can carry the HIV virus.

● Rimming (oral-anal contact) is not high risk for HIV transmission, but it is for hepatitis-B. Always use a latex barrier between the mouth and the anus – either a dental dam or a cut-up condom.

● When fisting, always use latex surgical gloves well-lubricated with plenty of water-based lubrication. Don't insert the fist past the length of the glove. Keep fingernails trimmed and smooth.

● Masturbating with a friend or in a group is not risky. Just make sure that semen is exposed only to unbroken skin. The same goes for 'water sports' (urinating on a partner). And never allow someone else's urine to get into your body through the mouth or the anus.

● Try not to share dildos and other sex toys. If you do, cover them with a new condom or scrub thoroughly each time somebody else uses them.

CHAPTER VIII

Especially for Young People

Young people face a triple whammy when it comes to HIV and AIDS. Consider:

● They have not heard and read about the disease for more than ten years, as adults have. And, since HIV takes so long to develop into full-blown AIDS, they probably do not know anyone who has it. As a result, the disease seems far off and distant – somebody else's problem.
● Kids think they are invincible anyway.
● And youth is the time when the hormones start to rage. Now combine this physiological awakening of sexuality with the fact that most kids aren't informed or mature enough to deal with it properly. (For adolescents and post-adolescents, sex can be anything from a casual recreational activity, to a way to 'prove' their

love, to a way to bolster their self-esteem, to a thing to do simply because it's considered 'cool'.) What you have is an extremely explosive combination.

The figures back this up. A study conducted in 1990 by the Centers for Disease Control found that 19 percent of American high-school students (and 27 percent of the boys) have had four or more sex partners, and that fewer than half of the sexually active students used condoms. To date, fewer than a thousand people aged thirteen to nineteen have been diagnosed with AIDS. But with behaviour like that going on, the number is sure to rise.

Some people have said that the best way to prevent such an epidemic is to promote abstinence. And abstinence has no bigger supporter than I. If you're a teenager and you're reading this book, first of all, I congratulate you for attempting to keep yourself informed. Second of all, I ask you to consider whether being sexually active is really the best course of action at this point in your life. Over and above all the issues related to HIV, I believe that most young people are simply not prepared to handle all the emotional baggage that comes with sex. You have many years ahead of you, years that will provide ample opportunity for sex. But you will never have a chance to be a kid again. 'Just say no' may be words to remember when it comes to sex, too.

Having said that, I understand that for many young people, a few words from Dr. Ruth are not going to be enough to convert them to a life of abstinence. If you are one of these people, I have one request to make of you: try as hard as you possibly can to limit your sexual activity to *safer* sex. If condoms are not available in your school, buy them at a drugstore – they're less expensive than a new cassette tape. In some countries, family planning organisations provide condoms free or for a nominal charge for young people.

Besides helping you avoid getting HIV, using condoms consistently and properly, as outlined in Chapter III, will greatly reduce the risk of pregnancy. And having a baby – the total responsibility of caring and providing for another human being – is something *no* teenager is prepared for.

I know it's hard to practise safer sex all the time. It's embarrassing to talk about, it takes away from the spirit of the moment, you may feel that it interferes with the pleasure you get out of sex. But the next time you're in school, take a look around the classroom. The chances are that at least a couple of kids in the room are infected with HIV. A little embarrassment or awkwardness is a small price to pay for avoiding this terrible disease. Taking a vow never to let yourself do unsafe sex is your best bet of making sure that *you'll* never be infected and that you'll live a long life filled with sex, love, and happy times.

The Joy of Safer Sex

As I was writing this book, I couldn't help being struck by some of the words I was using over and over again. *Disease. Risk. Never. Danger. Don't. Bodily fluids. Open sores.* That's not counting all the anatomical terms that might make shy folk blush. And, of course, there's the Big Chill itself. *Death.*

I don't apologise for any of it; it was necessary. When dealing with an epidemic of the magnitude of HIV and AIDS, it is absolutely essential that all the pertinent information gets put on the table, no matter how clinical, upsetting, or downright depressing it may seem.

At the same time, I hope I've made it clear that no matter how chilling the spectre of HIV/ AIDS is, we should not permit it to take over our lives – or even our sex lives. As the doctors work to find a cure – and to make the lives of the infected as pain-free, productive, and long as possible – it behoves all of us to remember that sex and love are still here, as full of possibility and magic as ever. It's just that, in this day and age, we have to be a little more creative. And a little more cautious.

Remember: This terrible disease has taken health and life away from so many people. Don't let it take away the joy of (safer) sex, too.

RESOURCE GUIDE

The following organisations provide advice and information on HIV and AIDS including telephone numbers of local and specialised helplines and suppliers of condoms and other safer sex aids.

IN AUSTRALIA

AFAO (AUSTRALIAN FEDERATION OF AIDS ORGANISATIONS)
GPO BOX 229, Canberra ACT 2061
62 47 3411

AIDS TRUST OF AUSTRALIA
58 Sophia Street, Surry Hills
2 211 2161
Raises money for education, help and care.

NATIONAL PEOPLE LIVING WITH AIDS COALITION
2 283 3535

IN NEW ZEALAND

NEW ZEALAND AIDS FOUNDATION
PO BOX 6663, Wellesley Street, Auckland
9 303 3124
HELPLINE (NATIONAL TOLL FREE NUMBER): 395 560
Services including support, care and education.

NPLWAIDS UNION
PO BOX 2558, Wellington
4 828 791
The national organisation for people living with
HIV/AIDS.

IN SOUTH AFRICA

AIDS HOTLINE
11 725 3009

AIDS EDUCATION AND INFORMATION
CENTRES
Durban 31 300 3104
Johannesburg 11 725 0551 ext 2098/2099/2102
Cape Town 21 448 7312

BODY POSITIVE
PO BOX 7258 Roggebaai, Cape Town 8012
PO BOX 17668, Hillbrew Johannesburg 2038.
Tel 11 720 5214

TOWNSHIP AIDS PROJECT
PO BOX 4168, Johannesburg 2000
982 5621/982 5810
Information, counselling, education and local training to
encourage community action against AIDS.

IN THE UNITED KINGDOM

NATIONAL AIDS HELPLINE
0800 567 123
Free 24 hour confidential service for any questions on
HIV/AIDS.

HEALTH EDUCATION AUTHORITY
Hamilton House, Mabledon Place, London WC1H 9JE
071 383 3833
Runs mass media campaigns and produces material to
support local HIV prevention.

NATIONAL AIDS TRUST
Euston Tower, 286 Euston Road, London NW1
071 388 1188
Coordinates and serves the voluntary sector.

TERRENCE HIGGINS TRUST
52–54 Grays Inn Road, London WC2
071 831 0330
Helpline 071 242 1010
Advice centre 071 831 0330
Offers a wide range of services which are open to everyone.

BODY POSITIVE
51b Philbeach Gardens, London SW5 9EB
071 835 1045
For people who are HIV Positive.

POSITIVELY WOMEN
5 Sebastian Street, London EC1V 0HE
Helpline 071 490 5515
For women with HIV and AIDS.

MAINLINERS
PO BOX 125, London SW9 8EF
071 274 4000 ext 443
For drug users.

BLACK HIV/AIDS NETWORK
111 Devenport Road, London W12 8PB
081 742 9223
For black people with HIV and AIDS.

HAEMOPHILIA SOCIETY
123 Westminster Bridge Road, London SE1 7HR
071 928 2020

AIDS AHEAD
144 London Road, Northwich, Cheshire CW9 5HH
0606 47046
For deaf people.

POSITIVE PARTNERS
8 Manor Gardens, London N7 6LA
071 249 6068
For partners of people infected with
HIV/AIDS.

FREE CONDOMS and lubricants can be obtained from
Family Planning Clinics, Brook Advisory Centres, certain
needle exchange and drug agencies, and from some GPs
and STD clinics.

Male and female condoms, lubricants and dental dams
can be obtained by mail order, from CONDOMANIA, 57
Rupert Street, London W1V 7HN. Tel 071 287 4540.

BIBLIOGRAPHY

Blank, Joani. *Good Vibrations: The Complete Guide to Vibrators*. San Francisco: Down There Press. 1989.

Breitman, Patti, Kim Knutson, and Paul Reed. *How to Persuade Your Lover to Use a Condom ... and Why You Should*. Rocklin, Cal.: Prima Publishing (distributed by St. Martin's Press). 1987. Brief paperback with some useful information and advice.

Dodson, Betty. *Sex for One: The Joy of Selfloving*. New York: Harmony Books. 1984. The last word in masturbation.

Douglas, Paul Harding, and Laura Pinsky. *The Essential AIDS Fact Book*. New York: Pocket Books. Revised edition, 1992.

Hein, Dr. Karen, and Theresa Foy DiGeronimo. *AIDS: Trading Fears for Facts. A Guide for Young People*. Yonkers, N.Y.: Consumer Reports Books. Revised edition, 1991.

Lacroix, Nitya. *Sensual Massage: An Intimate and Practical Guide to the Art of Touch.* New York: Henry Holt. 1989. Lavishly photographed.

Madaras, Lynda. *Lynda Madaras Talks to Teens About AIDS: An Essential Guide for Parents, Teachers and Young People.* New York: Newmarket Press, 1988. A very informative paperback.

Patton, Cindy, and Janis Kelly. *Making It: A Woman's Guide to Sex in the Age of AIDS.* Ithaca, New York: Firebrand Books. Revised edition, 1990. A useful pamphlet, in English and Spanish.

Preston, John, and Glenn Swann. *Safe Sex: The Ultimate Erotic Guide.* New York: New American Library. 1986. A spirited, gay-oriented handbook.

Rheingold, Howard. *Virtual Reality.* New York: Touchstone Books. 1992.

Whipple, Beverly, and Gina Ogden. *Safe Encounters: How Women Can Say Yes to Pleasure and No to Unsafe Sex.* New York: Pocket Books. 1990.

Zimet, Susan, and Victor Goodman. *The Great Cover-Up: A Condom Compendium.* New York: Civan, Inc. 1988. Everything you ever wanted to know.

INDEX